P9-CBA-401

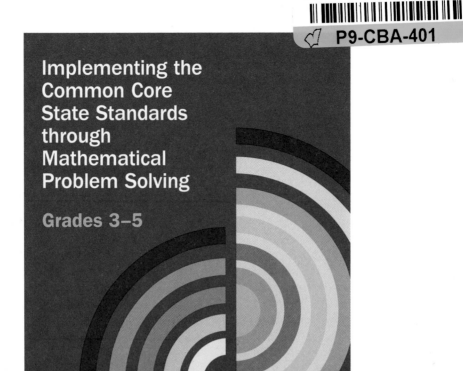

Implementing the Common Core State Standards through Mathematical Problem Solving

Grades 3–5

Mary Q. Foote
Queens College of the City University of New York

Darrell Earnest
University of Massachusetts Amherst

Shiuli Mukhopadhyay
California State University, Northridge

Frances R. Curcio, Series Editor
Queens College of the City University of New York

NATIONAL COUNCIL OF
TEACHERS OF MATHEMATICS

Copyright © 2014 by
The National Council of Teachers of Mathematics, Inc.
1906 Association Drive, Reston, VA 20191-1502
(703) 620-9840; (800) 235-7566; www.nctm.org
All rights reserved

Library of Congress Cataloging-in-Publication Data

Foote, Mary Q.
  Implementing the common core state standards through mathematical problem solving. Grades 3–5 / Mary
Q. Foote, Queens College of the City University of New York, Darrell Earnest, University of Massachusetts
Amherst, Shiuli Mukhopadhyay, California State University, Northridge; Frances R. Curcio, series editor,
Queens College of the City University of New York.
      pages cm
  Includes bibliographical references.
  ISBN 978-0-87353-724-7
  1. Problem solving—Study and teaching (Elementary) 2. Mathematics—Study and teaching (Elementary)
—Standards—United States. I. Foote, Mary, 1949 February 26– II. Mukhopadhyay, Shiuli. III. Curcio,
Frances R. IV. National Council of Teachers of Mathematics. V. Title.
  QA63.E24 2013
  372.7'049—dc23

                                                                        2013012288

The National Council of Teachers of Mathematics is the public voice of mathematics
education, supporting teachers to ensure equitable mathematics learning of the highest quality
for all students through vision, leadership, professional development, and research.

When forms, problems, and sample documents are included or are made available on NCTM's web-
site, their use is authorized for educational purposes by educators and noncommercial or nonprofit
entities that have purchased this book. Except for that use, permission to photocopy or use material
electronically from *Implementing the Common Core State Standards through Mathematical Problem
Solving: Grades 3–5* must be obtained from www.copyright.com, or contact Copyright Clearance
Center, Inc. (CCC), 222 Rosewood Drive, Danvers, MA 01923, 978-750-8400. CCC is a not-for-
profit organization that provides licenses and registration for a variety of users. Permission does
not automatically extend to any items identified as reprinted by permission of other publishers and
copyright holders. Such items must be excluded unless separated permissions are obtained. It will be
the responsibility of the user to identify such materials and obtain the permissions.

The publications of the National Council of Teachers of Mathematics present a variety of viewpoints.
The views expressed or implied in this publication, unless otherwise noted, should not be interpreted
as official positions of the Council.

Printed in the United States of America

Contents

Series Editor's Foreword

The purpose of *Implementing the Common Core State Standards through Mathematical Problem Solving: Grades 3–5,* as well as the other books in the series (those for kindergarten–grade 2, grades 6–8, and high school), is to (1) provide examples of how instruction that focuses on developing mathematical problem-solving skills supports the Common Core State Standards (CCSS), (2) help teachers interpret the Standards in ways that are useful for practice, and (3) provide examples of rich mathematical tasks and ways of implementing them in the classroom that have specific links to multiple standards. The books in this series are not meant to be comprehensive collections of mathematics problems for the entire school curriculum; instead, they contain rich problems and tasks of selected topics designed to develop several mathematics concepts presented in ways that illustrate the connections and interrelatedness between the Common Core and mathematical problem solving.

The Common Core State Standards for Mathematics

In June 2010, responding to the declining achievement of United States school children in reading and mathematics both nationally and internationally, the National Governors' Association Center for Best Practices (NGA Center) and the Council for State Chief School Officers (CCSSO) issued the *Common Core State Standards* (www.corestandards.org). The CCSS program is a unified, national effort to strengthen the ability of future citizens to be globally competitive, while preparing them for college and career readiness. The standards and practices across the grades are expectations for improving the teaching and learning of mathematics. Toward this concerted effort, a large majority of the states, along with the Washington, D.C., school system, have adopted the Common Core State Standards.

Similar to the standards in *Principles and Standards for School Mathematics* (National Council of Teachers of Mathematics 2000), the essential mathematics content in the Common Core State Standards for Mathematics (CCSSM) for grades 3–5 is included in several content areas ("domains") with various degrees of specificity: Operations and Algebraic Thinking, Number and Operations in Base Ten, Number and Operations—Fractions, Measurement and Data, and Geometry, with modeling expected to be integrated throughout the other content areas. An overview of the CCSS standards for mathematics in kindergarten through grade 5 is included in the appendix.

For each content area, the eight Standards for Mathematical Practice, which may be considered as fundamental elements of mathematical problem solving, are included as follows:

CCSS Standards for Mathematical Practice

MP.1 Make sense of problems and persevere in solving them.

MP.2 Reason abstractly and quantitatively.

MP.3 Construct viable arguments and critique the reasoning of others.

MP.4 Model with mathematics.

MP.5 Use appropriate tools strategically.

MP.6 Attend to precision.

MP.7 Look for and make use of structure.

MP.8 Look for and express regularity in repeated reasoning. (NGA Center and CCSSO 2010)

These practices are highlighted throughout the problem-solving tasks and activities contained in each of the books in this series.

Mathematical Problem Solving

Although problem solving has always been a goal of mathematics instruction, Pólya's helpful guide, *How to Solve It* (1957) had been in print for several decades before the publication of *An Agenda for Action* in 1980, in which the National Council of Teachers of Mathematics (NCTM) asserted the importance of mathematical problem solving in the school curriculum. That is, "*the mathematics curriculum should be organized around problem solving*" (NCTM 1980, p. 2, original in italics).

But what is mathematical problem solving? Throughout the years, although not research-based, instruction in developing mathematical problem-solving skills has relied on Pólya's (1957) four-step approach—understanding the problem, developing a plan, carrying out the plan, and looking back to determine whether the solution makes sense.

At the heart of the problem-solving process is determining what consists of a problem for learners of mathematics. Different from a familiar exercise or example for which learners have a prescribed approach for obtaining a solution, a "problem" is usually non-routine and nontraditional, and the learner needs to bring strategies, tools, and insights to bear in order to solve it (Henderson and Pingry 1953). In the late 1980s, textbooks and supplemental resource materials highlighted various problem-solving strategies to assist learners in approaching and solving problems. Such strategies as guessing and checking, using a drawing, making a table or an organized list, finding a pattern, using logical reasoning, solving a simpler problem, and working backward (O'Daffer 1988) became staples of mathematics instruction.

Much of the research on mathematical problem solving was conducted in the mid-1970s through the late 1980s (Schoenfeld 2007). The intent was not to focus on solving a given problem, but rather on examining how to help learners to develop strategies to tackle problems and real-world applications. Throughout the years, as attempts have been made to concentrate and manage the complexity of studying various aspects of mathematical problem solving, research attention has been redirected to mathematical modeling (Lesh and Zawojewski 2007; Lester and Kehle 2003). According to Henry Pollak:

> Problem solving may not refer to the outside world at all. Even when it does, problem solving usually begins with the idealized real-world situation in mathematical terms, and ends with a mathematical result. Mathematical modeling, on the other hand, begins in the "unedited" real world, requires problem formulating before problem solving, and once the problem is solved, moves back into the real world where the results are considered in their original context. (Pollak 2011)

The Common Core State Standards suggest that instruction in mathematics integrate modeling in mathematical tasks and activities, and they identify specific standards for which modeling is recommended, thus challenging teachers, curriculum developers, and textbook authors to bring authentic, real-world data into the classroom. Through mathematical problem solving and modeling, students' experience in mathematics will extend beyond traditional, routine word problems.

Recently, with its Essential Understanding (NCTM 2010–13) and Reasoning and Sense Making (NCTM 2009–10) series, NCTM has offered ideas to help teachers actively involve students in analyzing and solving problems. This newer series, Implementing the Common Core through Mathematical Problem Solving, contributes to these efforts, specifically supporting the connections between CCSSM and mathematical problem solving.

The authors of this book, Mary Q. Foote, Darrell Earnest, and Shiuli Mukhopadhyay, are gratefully acknowledged for sharing their insights and ideas to help elementary school mathematics teachers meet the challenges of implementing the Common Core State Standards. Thanks are due to the NCTM Educational Materials Committee for making the development of this manuscript possible, and to Joanne Hodges, senior director of publications, Myrna Jacobs, publications manager, and the NCTM publications staff for their guidance, advice, and technical support in the preparation of the manuscript.

Frances R. Curcio
Series Editor

Preface

All students, regardless of their personal characteristics, backgrounds, or physical challenges, must have opportunities to study—and support to learn—mathematics. (NCTM 2000, p. 12)

The Common Core State Standards for Mathematics (CCSSM) present an opportunity for teachers to receive added support in their efforts to raise expectations for all students, including those from groups that have traditionally been underserved in schools in general and in the study of mathematics in particular (DiME 2007; Martin 2006). The adoption and implementation of CCSSM may make it possible to achieve more equitable outcomes for all students. As it is stated in the discussion of the Equity Principle included in *Principles and Standards for School Mathematics* (National Council of Teachers of Mathematics [NCTM] 2000): "Well-documented examples demonstrate that all children, including those who have been traditionally underserved, can learn mathematics when they have access to high-quality instructional programs that support their learning" (Campbell 1995; Griffin, Case, and Siegler 1994; Knapp et al. 1995; Silver and Stein 1996). This section of *Principles and Standards* goes on to say, "Achieving equity requires a significant allocation of human and material resources in schools and classrooms. Instructional tools, curriculum materials, special supplemental programs, and the skillful use of community resources undoubtedly play important roles" (NCTM 2000, p. 14).

The goal of this book is to illustrate how the teachers of students in grades 3–5 can implement problem solving as they address relevant Common Core standards. This volume can be thought of as one set of instructional tools that can help teachers to achieve equity in their classrooms. The book includes thirty-eight tasks designed to be used by elementary school teachers in grades 3–5, as well as by teacher educators in mathematics methods classes and in professional development. Although we are focusing on grades 3–5 here, it is important to keep in mind how the content standards addressed in this book are positioned within the trajectory of topics from kindergarten to grade 12. Because of this, you will find that we attempt to link what we are doing in the content chapters to what has been previously done in the kindergarten–grade 2 band, and that we anticipate how the work of grades 3–5 will develop further in the grades 6–8 band.

The Common Core State Standards for Mathematics reflect a national effort to consider the needs of students in each grade, how to best support them before a given grade, and how a given grade prepares students for mathematics in subsequent grades. Understanding these standards in their entirety requires discussion among teachers and other educators about what the standards mean and how best to implement them. As teachers begin their journey with CCSSM, discussions in schools might center on what new opportunities these standards present for teachers and students alike. We hope this book will serve as an effective resource that helps teachers to make the most of these possibilities.

Chapter 1

Effectively Teaching to the CCSSM Standards

In this introductory chapter, we lay out a philosophy for the most effective way of teaching to the Common Core State Standards for Mathematics (CCSSM). This philosophy includes our beliefs about the importance of (*a*) an inclusive classroom environment, where the contributions of all students are valued; (*b*) the use of problem solving as a vehicle for engaging students in content within the structure of a three-part lesson format; and (*c*) engaging students with mathematics. The three sections of this chapter discuss these points in depth; the five chapters of the book that follow will show how to implement this philosophy in the classroom through thirty-eight tasks designed to meet specific CCSSM standards.

An Inclusive Classroom Environment

Even an engaging and approachable mathematics task is not sufficient to support student achievement, if it is not also accompanied by a classroom atmosphere that values all students, their contributions, and the knowledge they bring. Along with providing interesting and appropriately challenging tasks, it is critical to engage learners in the examination and discussion of mathematical ideas and processes. Students who do not participate are unlikely to learn (Lave and Wenger 1991).

One essential aspect of participation within the problem-solving lesson is the exchange of mathematical ideas through discussion. In order for students to be comfortable presenting their ideas to others, either in small groups or within whole-class discussions, the teacher must create a classroom environment where students feel able to take risks when presenting their thinking, even if their ideas are not fully developed. A classroom should be a place where it is safe to present this emergent thinking and acceptable to revise your thinking when other work that challenges any misconceptions is presented. Emergent thinking might include, for example, a misapplication of principles of operations of addition (add ones and tens) to multiplication of two-digit numbers (not applying the distributive property and thus only multiplying ones with ones and tens with tens). Misconceptions or erroneous answers can be positioned as an opportunity for learning by all, as they often reveal common ways that students make sense of complicated mathematics (e.g., see tasks 3.1 and 4.5) and show the importance of being open to revision (e.g., see task 3.6). Teachers need to support students in developing this willingness to revise thinking, as this process leads to more sophisticated understandings of various topics. In such an open classroom environment, students feel validated and appreciate that the contributions they bring to exploring and discussing mathematics are valued.

As we all know, learning does not happen just in school; it also occurs in other places that students inhabit, such as their homes and communities. In addition to respecting classroom contributions, valuing the knowledge that students bring with them to the classroom—and building on that knowledge—can also support student success. When teachers incorporate familiar home or community contexts into problem solving, this can support students' development toward meeting the CCSSM standards as they grapple with situations in which they are able to draw on their own knowledge (Moll et al. 1992; González et al. 2001). This placing of mathematics within a familiar context also increases the likelihood of equitable learning outcomes in the classroom. In this volume we have attempted to create problem contexts that are accessible to all children, but teachers should use their knowledge of their own students to modify problem contexts as necessary in order to insure that students are able to understand the tasks and find entry points to solve them (e.g., see task 3.6).

A Problem-Solving Approach

Building on the work of Van de Walle, Karp, and Bay-Williams (2010), all of the mathematics tasks in this book employ a problem-solving approach, which follows a three-part lesson format:

> Part 1: Launching the Task
>
> Part 2: Task Exploration
>
> Part 3: Summarizing Discussion

In **Launching the Task,** students are presented with a mathematical task that provides them with an opportunity to explore and engage with a particular CCSSM domain. During the launch, the teacher orients students to the task by focusing on three elements: (*a*) *task:* how students understand what a task is asking; (*b*) *engagement:* how students will engage in the exploration; and (*c*) *accountability:* how and in what capacity students will be accountable for demonstrating their thinking and problem solving. Problems can be launched in a variety of ways, such as discussing aspects of the problem that students might not understand fully without some whole-class conversation, reading a book that links to and supports understanding of the problem, brainstorming what students know or think about a particular topic, or linking the problem to some previous experience with mathematics.

In the **Task Exploration** part of the lesson, students have an opportunity to explore the target mathematics using relevant representations and working most often in pairs or in small groups. Students engage in working on (or exploring) the problem while the teacher circulates among groups or individuals, helping students to get started, conducting informal observations and assessments, and/or supporting student thinking with pertinent questions and comments. During this exploration period, teachers seek to understand the problem-solving approaches and mathematical thinking their students are using. In this way, teachers have an opportunity to prepare themselves for the summarizing discussion, during which several students or groups of students will present their thinking. Teachers should come to the exploration portion of the lesson having anticipated both correct and incorrect student responses to the task, and representations that students might use in their problem solving. In this way, they are better prepared to consider the range of ideas and representations that students will use during the exploration. Although they may not have anticipated each student response, through this advanced consideration of student responses, teachers are better prepared to interact thoughtfully with students to support their task exploration.

In the **Summarizing Discussion** that concludes the lesson, various solution paths that have been used to approach the problem are discussed. Connections are made between the mathematics and student thinking. It is during this time that more emergent strategies, such as direct modeling, can be linked to more sophisticated numeric strategies, thus supporting conceptual development. The summarizing discussion should be seen as a non-negotiable norm when it comes to a problem-solving lesson. Many times, teachers spend time on the launch and the exploration but then find the discussion portion of the lesson more difficult to include in the time allotted. This is unfortunate, as the discussion is a critically important part of the lesson. This is the part during which students make connections and then confirm, revise, or correct their thinking, including confronting misconceptions. These discussions are valuable in that they (*a*) support students in developing their metacognitive skills—that is, how to monitor their thinking in relation to situations; (*b*) allow students to understand how others can think differently, thus deepening their understanding that there are a variety of approaches possible to any given problem; and (*c*) support students in expanding their repertoire of problem-solving strategies. Not having a summarizing discussion can be detrimental to students' growth, as they may leave a problem-solving experience with misunderstandings that could have been addressed during discussion.

It is important that before students present their thinking in front of others, the teacher, during the earlier exploration section, has reviewed their work. Not all student work that is presented needs to be correct, as there is value in discussing emergent thinking on a topic. As mentioned previously, the teacher needs to have created a classroom environment in which it is safe to present emergent thinking and acceptable to revise thinking when other work that challenges misconceptions is presented. Exploring misconceptions must be positioned as a worthwhile enterprise. When students present work that the teacher cannot position as valuable and contributory, this can be embarrassing and consequently demoralizing for them, something that can seriously impact how they feel towards mathematics.

Fosnot and Dolk (2001) discuss how "contextual problems" can be a good way to "develop children's mathematical modeling of the real world" (p. 24). A problem-solving approach can be brought to bear on both contextualized problems (or what are often referred to as word problems) and bare number problems, or problems that are not set within a context. Problems that may have mathematical merit from an instructional perspective but might appear dry to students can often be given a simple context to make the problem more accessible to students. See, for example, how sample task B gives a context to the problem included in sample task A.

Sample Task A

Figure out what this point is called on the number line.

Fig. 1.1. Number line for sample tasks A and B

Circle the correct answer:

$\frac{2}{6}$ $\frac{2}{7}$ $\frac{1}{4}$ 2 $\frac{2}{4}$

How did you figure out the answer?

Sample Task B

A runner is running a one-mile race. He is currently where the arrow is pointing to on the number line in figure 1.1. How far along the way do you think he is?

(*a*) two-sixths   (*b*) two-sevenths   (*c*) one-fourth   (*d*) two   (*e*) two-fourths

Please explain why you chose your answer.

There are times, however, when it may be more practical or even advantageous to present students with a non-contextualized or bare number problem such as the one in sample task A (Saxe et al. 2007). Well-designed problems involving only bare numbers have the potential to engage students in puzzling over mathematical arguments, structure, and representations by inspiring their curiosity. In the case of sample task A, for example, the unequal intervals in the problem contradict students' expectations of number lines, provoking them to puzzle over the principles or rules that underlie a representation they may see every day. Within this volume, you will find both types of problems.

Engaging with Mathematics

As well as delineating the mathematical content to be addressed at each grade level, CCSSM also offers eight key mathematical practices in which students should engage. These eight Standards for Mathematical Practices build on the earlier work of the NCTM Process Standards (NCTM 2000) and the Strands of Mathematical Proficiency from *Adding It Up* (National Research Council 2001). In this book, we will highlight particular practice standards that are addressed by the thirty-eight included tasks. Not all practice standards will be highlighted within particular tasks, but within the volume as a whole all eight practice standards are discussed in relation to specific problems.

In the various content chapters, we have often taken an "across the grades" perspective in developing and explicating tasks for this band of grades 3–5. This is for a number of reasons. Not only are there teachers who are teaching multigrade classes, but it is also typical for teachers to have a wide range of abilities among students even in a single-grade class. As we know, development is uneven, and mathematical tasks are at their best when they have multiple entry points for students of varying levels. This also means that it is helpful if tasks can be solved using a variety of strategies in addition to numeric approaches. These can include direct modeling, which can take the form of using manipulatives or representing thinking through diagrams or drawings. This method of presentation makes the tasks accessible to a wider range of students, and it makes them more suitable for multiage settings as well as for classrooms with a range of learners. One important result of this is more equitable participation. Furthermore, we hope that our problems are such that they can be adapted by teachers for use at different grades. Although content standards shift from grade to grade, mathematical ideas are revisited from year to year as more complicated mathematical ideas are linked to ones learned previously.

Chapter 2
Operations and Algebraic Thinking

The word *algebra* has its roots in Arabic. Although much of what we today call algebra can be traced to Arabic/Islamic mathematics, algebra itself has roots that go back to the Babylonians. Algebraic thinking was initially expressed with prose statements that did not include symbolic notation. This was true until symbolic notation became more widely used in the sixteenth century.

The Operations and Algebraic Thinking domain of the Common Core State Standards for Mathematics (CCSSM) is featured in elementary grades beginning in kindergarten and continuing through grade 5. The standards in this domain underscore the critical work of exploring and recording mathematical patterns in operations. Noticing, exploring, and representing patterns support a robust understanding of number and operations and prepare students for formal algebra work in later grades. In the kindergarten–grade 2 band, the Operations and Algebraic Thinking standards focus on the properties and structure of addition and subtraction; the standards for grades 3–5 build upon this work as they emphasize the properties and structures of multiplication and division through critical analysis and reflection. Grade 6 introduces the Expressions and Equations domain, in which students begin to work with numeric expressions as entities unto themselves. A strong foundation in Operations and Algebraic Thinking supports students in their work with this domain in middle school and with the domains of algebra and functions in high school.

In this chapter, we draw upon a problem-solving approach that supports explorations of patterns through the strategic use of representations. Representations that well support this work include numeric expressions, arrays, tables, letter notation, and concrete materials and manipulatives. In order to develop algebraic and relational thinking, students must be able to make connections across representations and ask questions of representations. Opportunities to notice, express, and then record patterns using different representations including manipulatives allow students to explore and communicate the properties and structure of the operations.

The Common Core mathematics standards for grades 3–5 are organized by grade. As with other chapters in this book, we present tasks with an *across grade-level organization*, by which we mean that these tasks may be used in different grades. To coordinate the organization of the Common Core State Standards with the purpose of this book, we indicate specific standards we believe a task may address well, though we note that tasks are not restricted to the standards we have identified. With our across grade-level perspective, we hope to support teachers of students who have different ability levels or who are in multiage or multigrade contexts.

In organizing the standards across grade levels, we identify four distinct areas that cut across the Operations and Algebraic Thinking standards for grades 3–5, though these areas are not mutually exclusive. These four areas include (1) properties and structures of operations, (2) interpreting reasonableness, (3) generating patterns, and (4) syntax of expressions. Unlike other mathematical topics listed in CCSSM (such as Number and Operations—Fractions, which begins with unit fractions), these four areas do not imply a sequence of content. In this chapter, nine tasks are arranged by the above four categories (see table 2.1). In the far right column of the table, we highlight specific mathematical practices that are at play for each of the four areas, but it should be noted that any of the eight practice standards may also be at play in different amounts across the nine tasks.

Table 2.1
Content areas, grade-level standards, and mathematical practice standards met by the tasks in chapter 2

Content Areas	Tasks	Grade 3 Standards	Grade 4 Standards	Grade 5 Standards	Standards for Mathematical Practice
Properties and structures of operations	2.1	3.OA.1 3.OA.5			MP.1, MP.3, MP.7
	2.2	3.OA.5	4.OA.1	5.OA.2	
	2.3	3.OA.2 3.OA.3 3.OA.4 3.OA.6	4.OA.1 4.OA.2		
	2.4	3.OA.5 3.OA.6 3.OA.7	4.OA.1 4.OA.2 4.OA.4		
Interpreting reasonableness	2.5	3.OA.8	4.OA.3	5.OA.2	MP.3
	2.6	3.OA.8	4.OA.3	5.OA.2	
Generating patterns	2.7	3.OA.9	4.OA.5	5.OA.3	MP.7, MP.8
Syntax of expressions	2.8	3.OA.4 3.OA.8	4.OA.3 4.OA.5	5.OA.2 5.OA.3	MP.7, MP.8
	2.9			5.OA.1	

Properties and Structures of Operations

Students need opportunities to notice and explore patterns that underlie properties of operations and equations. Such opportunities support critical and flexible mathematical thinking. The Operations and Algebraic Thinking domain in grades 3–5 places a particular emphasis on noticing and exploring properties of multiplication and division. The four tasks presented here were chosen to support student reflection on the use of multiplication and division. The emphasis both in this particular category and throughout the Operations and Algebraic Thinking domain is not on computation, but rather on patterns that emerge from computation due to the structure of the operations (e.g., the inverse property of multiplication and division) or that are unique to one operation (e.g., any number multiplied by zero is zero, yet any number added to zero is that same number).

To engage productively in tasks that target standards in this category, students engage in *relational thinking*, which includes exploring expressions and equations in their entirety rather than procedures for calculation (Carpenter et al. 2005). For example, relational thinking allows one to evaluate that the product of 4×15 is half that of 8×15 without performing any calculation, because we know that 8 is twice 4. Such exploration involves first *noticing* patterns and then *sharing* or communicating these patterns (Russell, Schifter, and Bastable 2012). These patterns may then be represented in words or numeric expressions, or by using such manipulatives as multi-link cubes.

While not explicitly a part of the grades 3–5 standards, relational thinking is a core component of exploring the properties and structures of operations. This includes interpreting an expression such as 5×7 as 5 groups of 7 objects each (3.OA.1), or interpreting the product, 35, as 5 times as many as 7 and 7 times as many as 5 (4.OA.1). At the same time, relational thinking involves properties of multiplication, such as commutativity (e.g., $5 \times 7 = 7 \times 5$); distributivity (e.g., $8 \times 7 = 8 \times (5 + 2)$); and associativity (e.g., $3 \times 5 \times 2 = (3 \times 5) \times 2$, or $3 \times 5 \times 2 = 3 \times (5 \times 2)$) (3.OA.5).

Over the course of grades 3–5, students are engaged in multiplication and division work. Standards in grades 3 and 4 highlight exploration of the inverse property of multiplication and division, building on prior standards in grade 2 involving the inverse property of addition and subtraction. In all the tasks presented in this section, the primary purpose is to help students focus on multiplication situations in order to explore the inverse relationship of multiplication and division. This also involves conceptualizing division problems as unknown-factor problems since that explicitly engages students in examining the inverse relationship of multiplication and division (3.OA.6).

Task 2.1: Yasmin's Solution

Yasmin solved the problem 11×17 by making simpler problems. First she multiplied 10×10 to find 100, and then she multiplied 1×7 to find 7. She added $100 + 7$ to find 107. What do you think of Yasmin's strategy? What would you tell Yasmin to help her?

Launching the Task—The purpose of this problem is to engage students both in discussing and analyzing the conceptual structure that underlies the operation of multiplying two-digit numbers. To get students prepared to engage in this activity, a brief pre-discussion of a few of the relevant mathematical concepts such as associativity and/or partial products may be helpful for activating prior knowledge. A partial-products strategy for two-digit by two-digit multiplication can be powerful for students. While the standard algorithm may mask the place value manipulations involved in double-digit multiplication, a partial products approach involving multiples of 10 can highlight it. Factors can also be decomposed into smaller parts that are not multiples of 10. This may make it easier to manage computation and thus can be a strategic starting point. In addition, this problem is ripe for a discussion of commutativity and associativity.

To launch the task, present a problem with simpler numbers to which students know the product (e.g., 11 × 9). Present students with the open multiplicative array for 11 × 9 (see fig. 2.1).

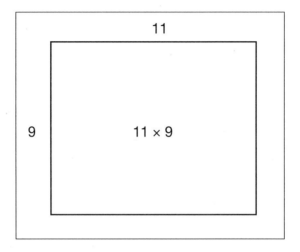

Fig. 2.1. Multiplicative array for 11 × 9

Then ask students how you might redraw the open array to show partial products. (*Note:* There are two partial products—10 × 9 and 1 × 9. These are added together to find the product of 11 × 9.) Show students how to draw an array to show that you first multiplied 10 × 9 and then 1 × 9. Does this array still show the product for 11 × 9? What are the different partial products to keep track of? The teacher might also use this opportunity to demonstrate how to draw arrays that will support students who might want to decompose 11 as 7 plus 4 or any other combination (see fig. 2.2). Children may lose track of the various partial products, and the arrays in figure 2.2 can help students represent and keep track of them.

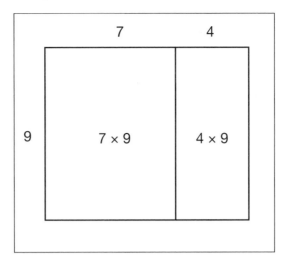

Fig. 2.2. Partial products arrays for 9 × 11

Task Exploration—To support students in task exploration, ask students to predict how they think Yasmin may have solved the problem. Where did the various numbers come from? Yasmin decomposed 11 into 10 and 1, and 17 into 10 and 7 before multiplying 10 × 10 and 1 × 7. Did she get all the right parts?

After their exploration, in pairs or small groups, students can return to the problem 11 × 17. As students are exploring and discussing, the teacher can walk around and ask students who are having difficulty getting started if there is an array they can draw to show 11 × 17, and if this could help Yasmin to prove she solved the problem correctly or help her to see whether she forgot to include some parts. If students are struggling, remind them of the multiplicative array for 11 × 9, and in particular draw attention to breaking down 11 into 10 and 1. To support students' work, ask them how they could use that to think about 11 and 17. Provide students with tiles if they need the support of direct modeling before transitioning to arrays. Figure 2.3 shows an array where 11 and 17 are decomposed along base-ten lines. Some students may in fact produce an array like this, but we are not suggesting that the teacher present this array to the class during the launch or exploration. If no student develops this array during the exploration, the teacher might consider introducing it during the discussion.

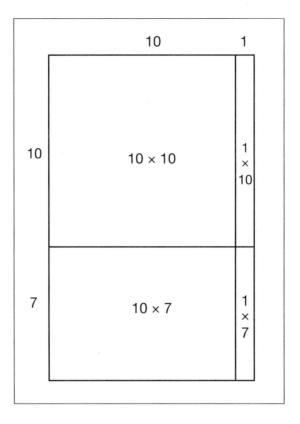

Fig. 2.3. Area model for 11 × 17 with factors decomposed along base-ten lines

Summarizing Discussion—To summarize students' work on the task, have several students present their thinking. Support a whole-class discussion to draw arrays to represent 11 × 17. Some students may decompose 10 and/or 17 into parts that map onto multiplication facts that they know or whose products can be easily arrived at by skip counting, such as (5 + 5) × (5 + 5 + 5 + 2). If none of the students offer the above array, the teacher may present it as a counter-suggestion, perhaps saying that she saw a student in another classroom solve the problem using that array. In this way, the teacher does not position herself as the most sophisticated knower of mathematics, a teaching move that may usurp some of the mathematical power from the students.

- How could we break down 11? How could we break down 17?
- How do we know we have all the partial products?
- Does the order in which we add the partial products matter? How do you know?
- Did Yasmin find all of the partial products? How do you think she forgot about 1 × 10 and 7 × 10?
- How is 11 × 9 different from 11 × 17?
- Would this still work if we multiply 17 × 11? How do you know?

With two-digit by two-digit multiplication, keeping track of the partial products is challenging. The multiplicative array is one representation that highlights the various partial products that need to be kept track of. Depending on their students' need, teachers may also consider using colored tiles as concrete manipulatives to help students construct the arrays. In examining various student arrays, the principle of associativity can be emphasized. When focusing on the final question and a discussion of associativity, it may be helpful for the teacher to have an 11 × 17 array made from a sheet of 1-inch grid paper and possibly laminated. This can then be rotated for a visual demonstration of commutativity.

Task 2.2: Comparing Expressions, Expressing Relations

Without doing any calculation, within each set (see table 2.2), what do you know about the relationship between the products for the given expressions? (Feel free to modify the numbers so that they are appropriate for your students.)

Table 2.2
Number sets for task 2.2

Set 1	4 × 15	8 × 15	4 × 30
Set 2	10 × 40	20 × 40	10 × 80
Set 3	20 × 150	40 × 150	20 × 300
Example	2 × 5	4 × 5	2 × 10

Launching the Task—The expressions in this problem are intended to support students' exploration of the *associative property of multiplication.* You may wish to launch this task either in a whole-group setting or by pairing students. If you are working in a whole-group context, write the example expressions on the board for all to see (see fig. 2.4). If you are pairing students, you can again write the expressions on the board or reproduce the expressions on a sheet of paper for each pair to consider. Allow students time to compare the expressions in figure 2.4.

Fig. 2.4. Example expressions to use in launching the task

Ask for volunteers to compare the expressions without calculating. In looking at the example set, students may compare the two leftmost expressions and see that 4 is twice as big as 2, and because 5 is the same in both expressions, 4 × 5 is twice as big as 2 × 5. As students volunteer their observations of the three expressions, record some of these observations on the board. Students may notice that 4×5 is half of 4×10. They may also notice that the final two expressions (e.g., 4×5 and 2×10) are equivalent.

Task Exploration—Review the expressions in sets 1, 2, and 3. These can be written on the board or reproduced on paper for students. Depending on your grade or students' prior knowledge, you may modify the numbers. Allow students time to explore with partners or in small groups. Pose the following question to students as they start their exploration:

- What do you know about these expressions?
- What do you notice?

Students may choose any method they like to record their observations on paper, including sentences in words (e.g., for set 3: 40 is twice as big as 20, so 40×150 is twice as big as 20×150) or as equations or inequalities (e.g., $2 \times (20 \times 150) = 40 \times 150$). Students can also be encouraged to use arrays or tiles for exploration of these relationships. Arrays are powerful representations to support this work, and they may be created with tiles or by using grid paper. In figure 2.5, an array of tiles displays how the product of 8×15 is twice that of 4×15, and how 8×15 is comprised of two sets of 4×15. Moreover, the product of 4×30 is equivalent to that of 8×15. Tiles may be moved in order to support this understanding; specifically, one set of the 4×15 array may be moved to below the other to represent 4×30, providing a concrete representation of $(2 \times 4) \times 15 = 4 \times (15 \times 2)$.

Summarizing Discussion—To summarize students' observations across the expressions, ask students to volunteer their observations. For example, you may ask the following questions:

- What did you notice about these expressions? (*Note:* While the term *expression* is not used extensively in grades 3–5, it is heavily used in grades 6–8, and hearing it in a class discussion can support mathematical vocabulary development.)
- Which product will be the **smallest**? Without telling us the product, how do you know?
- Which product will be the **greatest**? Without telling us the product, how do you know?
- What do we know about multiplication?

In discussion, support students' observations about the expressions. For example, students may notice that the first number in 8×15 is doubled in comparison to 4×15 just as the second number in 4×30 is doubled in comparison to 4×15; or, $(4 \times 2) \times 15 = 4 \times (2 \times 15)$. Keep in mind that students for whom such an activity is unfamiliar may need support and encouragement to share their observations.

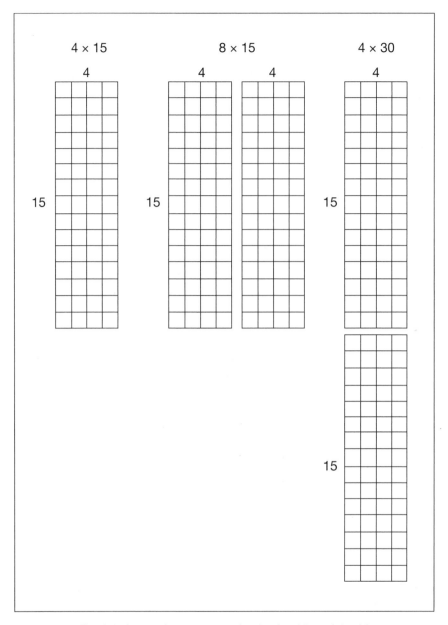

Fig. 2.5. Arrays that represent 4 × 15, 8 × 15, and 4 × 30

Task 2.3: Multiplicative Situations

Problems can be solved in different ways. How can you use multiplication and/or division to solve these problems? Explain your thinking.

> **Problem 1:** Liam is cooking potatoes. The recipe says you need 5 minutes for every pound you are cooking. How many minutes will it take for Liam to cook 12 pounds of potatoes?

Problem 2: Ms. Roper is making goodbye cards for her grade 5 students. She wants each card to be different from the others. She has 4 different colors of paper and 7 different stickers she can put on the paper. How many different cards can she make?

Problem 3: Nina can practice a song 5 times in an hour. If she wants to practice the song 60 times before the recital, how many hours does she need to practice?

Problem 4: Owen is building a rectangular tile patio that is 7 tiles wide and 4 tiles long. How many tiles does he need?

This task provides students with different multiplication or division situations, allowing them to explore different ways that the operations may be applied in story problems. (These particular tasks are adapted from ones found at a link at http://illustrativemathematics.org /illustrations/365.) Problems 1, 2, and 4 are each unknown product problems, while problem 3 is an unknown factor problem; problems 1 and 3 feature the same values, while problems 2 and 4 feature the same values.

Launching the Task—This task can be launched by engaging the class in a discussion of the four problem contexts so that students understand each. Students can be asked, for example, to share their own experiences with cooking vegetables, with making cards or books from construction paper, with practicing music or sports, and with building something at home or in school. While a number of students will not have had experiences with each context, there is likely to be at least a few with something to share about each. It is also fine to change the context of the task to one you think your students are more familiar with. If you do so, be sure not to change the underlying mathematics. After students have shared personal experiences with a similar context, you can lead a discussion examining the particular features of the problem context so that students are ready to begin the exploration.

Task Exploration—Allow students some time to explore the four problems either in pairs or in small groups. Alternatively, you may have different groups specialize in one or two of the situations. Depending on your instructional needs, you may even assign the four problems for homework to get students to do some thinking on their own. Ask students to explore and solve the problems in any way they feel most comfortable and confident. During the exploration phase, it is important that they feel successful in solving the problems using any strategy that works for them. It is not necessary to emphasize multiplication during the exploration phase. The focus on how to solve the problems using multiplication will be most valuable in the discussion phase after students have had an opportunity to solve the problem in their own way.

Encourage students to represent the situations in a variety of ways, including making drawings, using tiles or other manipulatives (e.g., creating an array of tiles to represent the patio in problem 4), or writing number expressions. If some students are attempting to solve the problem using repeated addition or repeated subtraction, that should also be encouraged. To prepare for the summarizing discussion, you may choose to have students record their thinking on large poster paper and then engage students in a gallery walk to consider how other groups represented the situations before engaging in a whole-class discussion.

Summarizing Discussion—Once students have had the opportunity to represent the situations, organize the class into a whole group for discussion. Provide students with an opportunity to share strategies for solving the above problems. In the first problem, for example, students may have used repeated addition to solve the problem ($5 + 5 + 5 + 5 + 5 + 5 + 5 + 5 + 5 + 5 + 5 + 5$) or they may have used multiplication ($5 \times 12 = \square$). Note that problem 3 is a missing factor problem that involves (or could involve) division as well as more emergent strategies such as skip counting. In particular, support students in comparing the problems above.

- How are problems 1, 2, and 4 alike?
- How is problem 3 different from the other problems?

During the discussion phase, instead of representing the result of the expression numerically, consider using a box to represent the unknown amount, so that eventually you have the following expressions displayed on the board (see fig. 2.6). Writing equations in this way provides students with the opportunity to engage in an examination of the numeric relationships between and among the expressions.

Fig. 2.6. Using a box to represent an unknown quantity

The values in this particular task allow teachers to lead the discussion in a couple of different directions. Compare $5 \times 12 = \square$ and $5 \times \square = 60$ to engage students in a discussion about the inverse property of multiplication and division. Alternatively, you may use $4 \times 7 = \square$ and $7 \times 4 = \square$ to engage students in considering the multiplicative property of commutativity. As you ask the last question above, draw students' attention to $5 \times \square = 60$. This problem may be written as a multiplication problem with a factor unknown, or as division problem.

To help students make connections to multiplication problem structures, the following questions can be helpful:

- Can we represent this situation using multiplication?
- What is an expression that shows this situation?
- What is the same or different about these solutions?

Task 2.4: Is Penelope Correct?

Penelope has just calculated 3 × 7 = 21. She thinks that the product for 4 × 7 is going to be 3 more than the product for 3 × 7. What do you think Penelope is thinking? Do you agree or disagree? With a partner, use drawings, multi-link cubes, or any other way you choose to help Penelope.

Launching the Task—Show students the equation 4 + 2 = 6. Below it write 5 + 2 = □ and ask them what goes in the box. Because of work they have done in kindergarten–grade 2, students may have understandings about the fact that when an addend is increased by 1 (such as changing the 4 from 4 + 2 to a 5 in 5 + 2) the sum also increases by 1. It may be helpful for students to hear that such thinking, without actual calculations, can sometimes be called *relational thinking*. After a discussion of their understanding of this idea, explain to students that in this task they will explore whether something similar is true for multiplication.

Task Exploration—Present the task for students by writing 3 × 7 and 4 × 7 on the board. To explore the problem further, students should work in small groups or pairs to create an argument for Penelope as to why 4 × 7 is not 3 more than 3 × 7. As you circulate around the room, encourage students to use drawings including arrays, manipulatives (such as multi-link cubes), or written language to convince Penelope. The goal is not for students to arrive at the products of 4 × 7 and 3 × 7. Rather, the goal is to engage students in an exploration that will support a subsequent discussion on the aspects of grouping during multiplication that can help students understand the distributive property of multiplication over addition. Some students, such as those who may think of 3 x 7 in terms of repeated addition (3 + 3 + 3 + 3 + 3 + 3 + 3), may believe that an additional 3 needs to be added to the product of 3 × 7 to solve 4 × 7. One important aspect of the operation of multiplication that differentiates it from the operation of addition is distinguishing between the groups and the number of objects in each group. Arrays can be a powerful tool for students to keep track of the number of groups and the number of items in each group as organized in the form of rows and columns (see fig. 2.7).

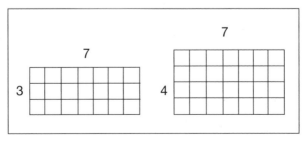

Fig. 2.7. Arrays can help distinguish between the number of groups and the number of objects within groups.

Summarizing Discussion—Once students have had an opportunity to create an argument for Penelope, have them share their ideas in a whole-class discussion. It is important for students to consider how the product changes when one of the factors increases by one (or by some other number). This prepares students for understanding more formally that $7 \times 4 = (7 \times 3) + (7 \times 1)$. Consider asking the following questions to begin the discussion.

- Do you agree with Penelope? Why or why not?
- How could you convince someone in another classroom that 4×7 is not 3 more than 3×7?
- What do you think Penelope was thinking? Has anyone here ever made that mistake?
- What is an expression that really is 3 more than 3×7? What would an array for that look like? How is that different from the array for 4×7?

For the final question above, support students in considering how to add 3 more to the array for 3×7, such as in figure 2.8.

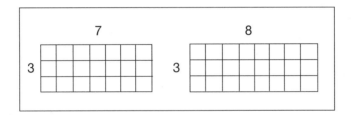

Fig. 2.8. Arrays for 3 × 7 and 3 × 8

STANDARDS *for Mathematical Practice—Tasks 2.1 through 2.4*

MP.1

The first Standard for Mathematical Practice states, "Make sense of problems and persevere in solving them" (National Governors Association Center for Best Practices and Council of Chief State School Officers [NGA Center and CCSSO] 2010, p. 6). Each of the four tasks requires students to make sense of the problems. In tasks 2.1 and 2.4, students are trying to make sense of how someone else was thinking about a problem and how that compares to the actual problem solving. In tasks 2.2 and 2.3, students are trying to make sense of the structures of tasks and problems analyzing similarities and differences.

MP.3

"Construct viable arguments and critique the reasoning of others" (NGA Center and CCSSO 2010, p. 6). In the four tasks presented above, students are expected to justify their conclusions, communicate them to others, and respond to the arguments of others. The tasks also allow students to construct arguments by drawing upon representations and numeric expressions. Further, while engaging in the summarizing discussion students are expected to listen to the arguments of others, decide whether they make sense, and ask useful questions to clarify or improve the arguments.

MP.7

"Look for and make use of structure" (NGA Center and CCSSO 2010, p. 8). The tasks presented above focus on the properties of multiplication. In each task, students reflect on the underlying structure of multiplication by translating across representations.

Interpreting Reasonableness

As students learn number facts and computation, procedures at times may overshadow important conceptual work involving evaluation and estimation using number sense. Across grades 3–5, the Common Core emphasizes students interpreting the reasonableness of expressions and equations. Such work engages students in critical aspects of numeric reasoning and relational thinking. This work may involve interpreting the meaning of a remainder and determining how best to represent that remainder given a particular context (4.OA.3). This work also involves mental computation and estimation to promote reflection on reasonableness of answers given what students already know about the number system and operations (3.OA.8, 4.OA.3, 5.OA.2).

One of the first aspects of division that students learn is that, when there is a remainder, its value cannot be greater or equal to the divisor. Yet students often understand the remainder as devoid of context. In this treatment, the remainder is simply the result of a division problem for which the divisor was not a factor of the dividend, and students record the remainder using the letter R and a numeric value; in such cases, the remainder is treated as separate from the divisor. Each of the three story problems below results in a remainder, yet each problem is different in how that remainder is treated. The situation in task 2.5 provides students an opportunity to develop a conceptual foundation for remainders in division, and helps them in interpreting the reasonableness of answers within specific problem contexts.

Task 2.5: Interpreting Remainders

Problem 1: The fourth- and fifth-grade students at Squantum Elementary School are going on a field trip. There will be 130 students going on the field trip. Each school bus fits 40 students. How many school buses do they need?

Problem 2: Ms. Davis is giving balloons to her kindergarten students. She wants to make sure that all students have the same number. She has 15 kindergarten students and 34 balloons. How many balloons will each kindergartner get?

Problem 3: Joe made brownies for himself and his friends to share equally. There are 12 brownies and 8 people total. How many brownies will each person get?

Launching the Task—To get the students prepared for the problem, teachers may wish to have a discussion about context and how that impacts the solution of a problem and what a reasonable answer is. For example, teachers may want to discuss how many cars would be reasonable for transporting 8 or 9 people. Another discussion point could be the types of things that can be further divided (such as cakes or brownies) and items that cannot be divided (such as toys or balloons). After the initial discussion, teachers may launch the tasks suggested above. Depending on the students, the teacher may present all three problems together. Teachers may also wish to present students with the same problems with friendlier numbers (e.g., 90 students instead of 130 to make calculations easier).

Task Exploration—Students may briefly work on the problem individually first and then come together in pairs or in a small group. Alternatively, students may start in pairs or small groups and explore together. Some students may consider the problem context as they determine their answers, while others may write expressions using the notation for remainders. Encourage students to use drawing or manipulatives to get a clearer understanding of the contexts. While circulating around the classroom, teachers might give students hints wherein they highlight aspects of each of the contexts above, helping students determine whether students need to round up (problem 1), round down (problem 2), or interpret the remainder as a fraction (problem 3). For example, if students find a remainder for the school bus problem, ask them how many buses they need. Can we have $1/4$ (or, remainder 10) of a school bus? For students who find a remainder for the balloon problem, ask them how many balloons each kindergartner receives. To help students find the remainder of the brownie problem, ask guiding questions about how many brownies each person receives or if the leftover brownies could be shared. Because brownies can be cut into fractional units, students should consider the remainder in terms of fractions of brownies.

Summarizing Discussion—Once students have had a chance to explore the different contexts and think about how to treat the remainders, bring the class together for a summarizing discussion. Focusing the discussion on important aspects of the problem will be helpful. In problem 1, the school needs 3 school buses to carry 120 of the students, but they still have 10 students who need to be on a bus; as a result, one needs to round up to 4 school buses in total. Note that an answer of $3^1/4$ is meaningless in such a context, as school buses cannot be divided. In problem 2, each student will receive 2 balloons, yet there are still 4 balloons left. Because Ms. Davis wants to ensure each kindergartner receives the same number of balloons, she does not distribute the remaining balloons (perhaps saving them for another class or her own children). As in problem 1, an answer of $2^2/3$ balloons is meaningless given the context. Unlike school buses and balloons, the brownies in problem 3 may be divided into fractional amounts. For this reason, the remainder takes on a different meaning. In this case, each child receives $1\frac{1}{2}$ brownies. The following questions can be helpful for conducting the discussion.

- How did you solve the school bus problem? Did anyone do it another way?
- How did you solve the balloon problem? Did anyone do it another way?
- How did you solve the brownie problem? Did anyone do it another way?
- How are these problems similar? How are they different?
- What did you notice about the remainders in each of the problems?
- Why do we treat the remainder differently in each problem?

Task 2.6: Kevin and Glenn Estimate

Kevin and Glenn are trying to estimate the product of 19×9. They disagree on who has the best estimate. Glenn estimated the product to be 180, while Kevin's estimate is 190. What do you think each boy was thinking? How did each boy arrive at his estimation?

Launching the Task—Estimation is a critical skill. This task engages students in considering estimation approaches. To launch the task, have students read the problem aloud and/or write the problem on the board. In this problem, the numbers chosen were intended to be more difficult for students to calculate mentally (or recall as facts). Both estimates are reasonable, and they are different from one another because of the different strategies chosen. Continue the launch by having students brainstorm different strategies that they use for estimation.

Task Exploration—Once students have had an opportunity to get their thoughts together, they may be asked to discuss what they think Glenn's and Kevin's strategies are, and how these strategies are different from one another. Some students may want to calculate the precise product, yet the emphasis of this problem is on estimation strategies. In such cases, the teacher should encourage and remind students about the goal of the task being to explore estimation. For situations in which an extension of the problem seems warranted, consider asking the following question:

- What if Norman estimated that 19×9 was close to 90, because 10×9 is 90? Do you think that is a good estimate? Why or why not?

Summarizing Discussion—The summarizing discussion should focus on strategies for estimating, such as rounding to a multiple of ten or another friendly number. Consider posing the following questions to students:

- What was Glenn's strategy? Let's have a volunteer to write this on the board.

- What was Kevin's strategy? Let's have a volunteer to write this on the board.
- Do you think Glenn had an efficient estimation strategy? What do you think about Kevin's strategy?

As students discuss their ideas, emphasize that a goal of estimation is not necessarily to reach the correct response. If this were the case, someone could calculate the product using paper and pencil or a calculator. Rather, estimation uses what we know about the number system to get a ballpark idea of an answer. Given our estimate, we may go back to the original problem in order to check the reasonableness of that estimate.

STANDARDS *for Mathematical Practice—Tasks 2.5 and 2.6*

MP.3

"Construct viable arguments and critique the reasoning of others" (NGA Center and CCSSO 2010, p. 6). In the two tasks presented in this section, students are expected to justify their conclusions, communicate them to others, and respond to the arguments of others. Forming mathematical arguments in order to interpret remainders (task 2.5) or consider the properties of a "good" estimate (task 2.6) is nontrivial. Students benefit from tasks that allow them to engage in such arguments, both through forming their own arguments and listening to the arguments of others.

Generating Patterns

Standards for generating and analyzing patterns cut across grades 3, 4, and 5. Standards that we group under this heading reflect exploring patterns of operating by a particular value (e.g., any number times 4 results in an even number; 3.OA.9). Furthermore, standards focus on functional relations, or input-output relations, such as generating a number sequence using the rule "add 3" and the starting number 1 (4.OA.5), or generating two numerical patterns using two rules, such as "add 3" and "add 6" with the starting number 0 and then comparing terms in the sequence (5.OA.3).

In the following problem (adapted from Carraher, Schliemann, and Schwartz 2008), students are introduced to a story context for which there is no one solution. This problem is appropriate for students across grades 3–5. One emphasis of task 2.7 is on generating a verbal expression to describe the relation of John's candies to Maria's candies, even if the problem does not state how many candies John and Maria have inside their boxes.

Task 2.7: The Candy Box Problem

John and Maria each have a box of candies, with the same number of candies in each box. Maria also has 3 candies on top of her box. Who has more candy? Will that always be the case if the number of candies inside the boxes changes? For example, what if John and Maria had 4 candies in their boxes? What if John and Maria had 6 candies in their boxes? Describe the situation with John and Maria's candies using words, drawings or manipulative materials, or numbers.

Launching the Task—In a whole-group context, pose the problem to students and encourage them to elaborate what they think it means. In order to do this, engage them in a discussion that addresses the following question: "What do you know about the number of candies that John and Maria each have?" To support further engagement in the task, present the class with two boxes (such as a recipe card box), one to represent John's candies and one to represent Maria's candies, with 3 candies taped to the outside of Maria's box. Engage students in considering how many candies they think may be inside the box. Students may offer their ideas based on the problem context, while others may wish to hold or shake the box of candies in order to estimate the number inside each.

Task Exploration—In order to support students' exploration of the task, you may question students during the exploration as to different possible quantities. For example, what if John has 3 candies? How many would Maria have? What if John has 4 candies? 5 candies? With each contribution, ask students whether it is a possibility based on what we know about John's candies and Maria's candies. Any response for which Maria has 3 more candies than John satisfies the problem context, while any response that does not maintain the difference of 3 violates that context. As students work on representing what they know about John's and Maria's candies, walk around the classroom and ask students how they know that what they are proposing is possible. As the task statement indicates, students may wish to draw pictures with particular numbers of candies, use numeric expressions, or represent the relation in some other way.

Summarizing Discussion—After students have had an opportunity to consider the total number of candies that John and Maria have, ask students to volunteer suggestions for possible values. The numeric pattern that underlies this problem supports students' understanding of a functional relation in which an input (John's total candies) corresponds to an output (Maria's total candies). Noticing and sharing the pattern in the Candy Box problem allows students to describe the relation of John's candies to Maria's candies even though we do not know how many candies are inside each box.

One way to organize these suggestions is to begin a table for which the first column represents John's candies and the second column represents Maria's candies. With each suggestion, ask students whether those values are possible given the problem. Record students' ideas in a table similar to table 2.3, only without the right-hand column labeled "Difference." After several students have contributed their ideas, students may notice (or you may need to draw attention to this by careful questioning) that many (or all) of the suggestions are different from each other, yet all have the same additive difference of 3. This may be a good point to add the third column indicating the difference of 3.

Table 2.3
Example of table for recording student responses

	John's candies	Maria's candies	Difference
Ana	5	8	3
Camille	10	10 + 3	3
David	11	14	3
Sofia	100	103	3
Mara	0	3	3
Susana	50	50 + 3	3

Consider representing some of Maria's values in the table as an unexecuted expression of the number of candies inside the box plus 3 (e.g., John has 10, Maria has 10 + 3; John has 50, Maria 50 + 3). The unexecuted expressions (10 + 3 and 50 + 3) preserve the relationship of the quantity that changes (the number of candies inside the box) along with the number that stays the same (the 3 candies on top of Maria's box). Encourage students to think about a way to describe all of the different ideas that work. The emphasis is on generating a verbal expression that captures that John and Maria have the same number of candies inside their boxes, but Maria always has 3 more candies than John.

- How many candies are inside John's box? Maria's box?
- How many candies would John have in total? How many would Maria have in total?
- How can all of these ideas be possible if they are all different? Is there anything that is the same about these ideas?

In addition to generating verbal expressions to capture the generalization, task 2.7 provides a context to introduce notation to represent the number of candies inside the box. You may wish to represent the number of John's and Maria's candies as □ and □ + 3, respectively. Alternatively, you may use letter notation to represent the number of candies inside the box (e.g., John has n, and Maria has $n + 3$). This idea is further elaborated in the next section on the syntax of expressions.

STANDARDS *for Mathematical Practice—Task 2.7*

MP.7

"Look for and make use of structure" (NGA Center and CCSSO 2010, p. 8). This standard also asks students to "look closely to discern a pattern or structure." Task 2.7 provides a useful context for this practice standard. The additive pattern in the Candy Box problem may be far from obvious without an appropriate classroom discussion to bring this out.

MP.8

"Look for and express regularity in repeated reasoning" (NGA Center and CCSSO 2010, p. 8). This standard includes noticing whether "calculations are repeated" and looking for "general methods and for shortcuts." In task 2.7, the activity is structured to highlight the additive pattern to describe the relationship of John's and Maria's candies. This regularity supports students' understanding of two related quantities and how to express that regularity in both specific values and general terms.

Syntax of Expressions

A theme of the Operations and Algebraic Thinking domain is relational thinking and patterns in expressions and equations. Along with this theme, the domain focuses explicitly on the syntax used in expressions and equations. By syntax, we mean the use and meaning of particular symbols. This includes the use of boxes or placeholders (e.g., □ or ?) to represent an unknown (3.OA.4) and the use of parentheses, brackets, and braces in expressions (5.OA.1). This also includes the use of letter notation across these grades (3.OA.8, 4.OA.3, 5.OA.2). The first task presented in this section (a variation of a problem in De Guirre 1980) provides students with an opportunity to explore such patterns and an opportunity to meaningfully introduce letter notation. The second task, directed at a grade 5 standard (5.OA.1), targets the syntax used in equations, specifically the role of parentheses.

Task 2.8: The Dinner Tables Problem

In your restaurant, square dinner tables are always arranged together in a straight line. Only one person may sit at a side of a single table. What is the greatest number of people that may sit at one table? Two tables? Three tables? What if the restaurant was going to seat an extremely large number of people at 10 tables? 50 tables? 100 tables? (Carraher, Martinez, and Schliemann 2008; Earnest and Balti 2008)

Launching the Task—In order to prepare students to work on this task, engage them in a conversation about their experiences at restaurants, with a focus on the types of tables that various restaurants have. Talk about whether they have ever been in a restaurant where two or more tables have been pushed together to make space for a larger party of people dining. Explain that this is what this restaurant does to accommodate parties larger than four people.

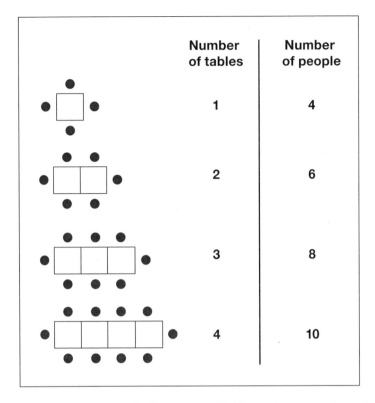

Number of tables	Number of people
1	4
2	6
3	8
4	10

Fig. 2.9. Table configurations with the number of tables and number of people noted

Task Exploration—As students get the idea of what they are expected to do, give them some time to explore on their own. Remind students that they can use manipulatives such as colored tiles or a drawing of the table configurations and people sitting around them, such as in figure 2.9. Encourage them to do this for three, four, or five tables. Continuing to represent new configurations of tables as drawings provides students with an opportunity to consider the patterns and regularity underlying the context (see fig. 2.10). We are not suggesting that teachers present this representation to the class at this point; instead, we provide it as an example of representations that students might develop during the exploration. Students may choose to draw each table and count the number of people in order to determine the total number of people. They may begin to notice that as each dinner table is added, the total number of people increases by 2. To engage students in extending the pattern, ask them to predict the total number of people that may sit at 10 tables.

Ask students to predict how many people would sit at 10 tables or 50 tables or 100 tables. For each of these (especially 50 and 100), drawing each and every table and counting the total number of people is laborious enough to provoke many students to consider a rule to move from the total number of tables to the total number of people that may sit there. As you circulate around the room to check in with students, ask them where they see the total number of people in their drawing or configuration of tiles.

Strategic use of representations draws attention to the underlying structure of the joint variation of the number of dinner tables to the total number of people. For example,

27

students may determine that for 5 tables, a total of 12 people may sit. In addition to writing the numeral 12, they may write and speak the unexecuted sum of numbers that corresponds to the drawing: 5 on top, 5 on the bottom, and 2 on the sides (Earnest and Balti 2008). When this pattern is consistently applied, students begin to consider the commonalities across examples. In this case, the unexecuted expression supports a connection between the drawing of dinner tables and the functional relation ($2n + 2$) at play. With specific reference to the problem context, for 4 tables, 4 people sit on top, 4 on the bottom, and then 2 on the sides. This same pattern applies to 10 tables, 100 tables, or any number of tables.

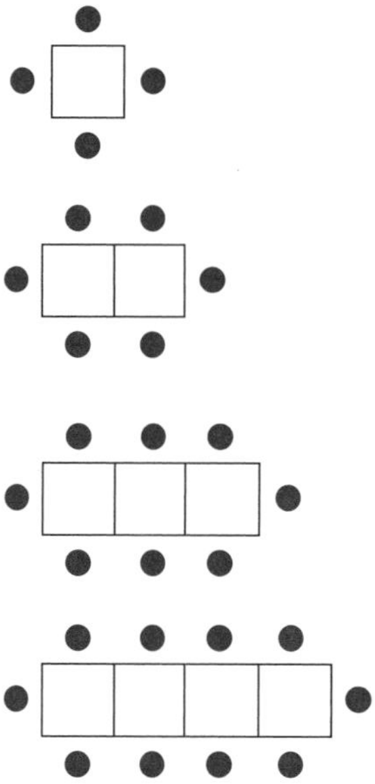

	Number of tables	Number of people	
	1	4	
	2	6	
	3	8	3 + 3 + 2
	4	10	4 + 4 + 2
	5	12	5 + 5 + 2
	10	22	10 + 10 + 2

Fig. 2.10. Possible representations for number of tables, number of people, and numerical expressions that represent the number of people

Summarizing Discussion—For the summarizing discussion, you may want to record student thinking on a chart similar to figure 2.9. As students contribute values, they can be added to the chart. You may wish to use this opportunity of recording student responses to introduce a letter notation to represent any number of tables. If you are introducing letter notation for the first time, you may want to engage students in conversation about what a particular letter, like *n*, may stand for. Some students may find a number beginning with that letter, like *9, ninety,* or even *none.* Support students' understanding through the use of academic language around letter notation. For example, "If *n* stands for 10 tables, how many total people are there? If *n* stands for 5 tables, how many total people are there?" Draw upon examples that have come up thus far in the discussion to model language that can support the generation of a rule. For example, if there are 10 tables, we have 10 people on top, 10 on the bottom, and 2 on the sides. If we have 100 tables, we have 100 on top, 100 on the bottom, and 2 on the sides. At the same time, record the unexecuted expressions: 5 + 5 + 2; 10 + 10 + 2; 100 + 100 + 2. Using this model, support students in noticing that if we have *n* tables, we have *n* + *n* + 2. To close the lesson, ask students the following questions.

- How many total people could sit at 4 tables? 5 tables? How many do you think could sit at 6? How do you know?

- How did you use drawings or tile representations of the tables and people to help determine the total number?

- Did anyone discover the total number of people at 10 tables without drawing out the tables and counting the people? What was your strategy?

- Can anyone think of a rule to describe how to find the total number of people, even if we do not know exactly how many dinner tables there are?

In most classrooms there is likely to be a range of responses involving general rules to describe the function. Support students in understanding that we know something about the total number of people even if we do not know exactly how many tables there are.

Task 2.9: Wacky Parentheses

Naima's grandmother is going to double Naima's money. Naima started with $4, and she then earned $6 more. Naima expected to have $20 total after her grandmother doubled her money. Her grandmother thought that Naima would have $14 (see fig. 2.11). How was Naima thinking about it? How was her grandmother thinking about it?

Naima's work 2 × 4 + 6 = 20	Her grandmother's work 2 × 4 + 6 = 14

Fig. 2.11. Naima and her grandmother's work

Launching the Task—Mathematical conventions, such as the use of parentheses or the order of operations, support our ability to communicate mathematical ideas to one another. In the task above, similar numeric expressions are set equal to different amounts. In the first case of Naima's work, she added the $4 and $6 together first and then multiplied that product by 2 to get $20. Nonetheless, the written expression lacks parentheses, and based on mathematical convention it was executed improperly. Her grandmother, on the other hand, executed the same expression according to convention (perform multiplication first and then addition), thereby setting it equal to a different amount. To launch the task, engage students in a conversation about their experiences earning money or receiving money as gifts. Ask them whether someone in their family has ever been as generous as Naima's grandmother was in offering to double her money. Next ask students to evaluate the following two expressions: $(2 + 1) \times 5$ and $5 + (2 \times 1)$. Engage them in a conversation about their knowledge of parentheses and elicit thinking about performing calculations within parentheses first.

Task Exploration—Ask students to work with partners to discuss how Naima and her grandmother solved the problem. Many students in grades 3–5 can easily calculate such a problem, yet may write the numeric expression as Naima did, or as a succession of calculations that misuses the equal sign (e.g., $4 + 6 = 10 \times 2 = 20$). As you circulate around the room, ask students whether they agree with Naima or her grandmother. Note that based on the original context, Naima's response is accurate; yet, based on the numeric expression, her grandmother's calculation is accurate. Ask students how they might rewrite the expression to make sure Naima receives the correct amount of money.

Summarizing Discussion—Ask students to share their numeric expressions, write them on the board, and then use these expressions to engage the class in discussion about the different ways students wrote them. You may choose to ask students the following questions:

- Whom do you agree with, Naima or her grandmother? Why might Naima be right? Why might her grandmother be right?
- How could you rewrite this expression to make sure Naima receives her money?
- What do you think parentheses mean when we use them in math? Are they necessary?

Let students know that as a way to deal with the very problem that Naima and her grandmother faced, mathematicians use parentheses in such expressions. As an extension or in order to assess students' understanding, you may create additional equations (with or without a context) for students to determine whether the two sides really are equal and, if not, where to add parentheses in order to make the two sides of the equation equal.

This task highlights the role of notation in such expressions, and it supports students in considering the implications of using notation in written expressions. Rather than memorizing rules for the order of operations or for how to execute an expression with parentheses, this task uses a story context to juxtapose two differently executed expressions and support students' considerations of when and why parentheses may be useful. The numbers in this problem are meant to be accessible to students, yet teachers should also feel free to alter values based on their knowledge of students in their classrooms.

STANDARDS *for Mathematical Practice—Tasks 2.8 and 2.9*

MP.7

"Look for and make use of structure" (NGA Center and CCSSO 2010, p. 8). Both tasks presented in this Syntax of Expressions section engage students in considering the underlying structure of written expressions. Task 2.8, the Dinner Tables problem, engages students in finding patterns of change as dinner tables are added. Students may notice patterns of change in different ways. For example, some may notice that in the table the total number of people increases by 2 as one additional table is added on. At the same time, with the use of unexecuted expressions and the drawing of the tables, students may notice that with each additional table, there is an added person at the top and another at the bottom; meanwhile, there are always only two people on either end of the table setup. In task 2.9, Wacky Parentheses, the structure of written expressions is explored with expressions that omit parentheses, demonstrating that the teaching of conventions does not need to depend on simple memorization. Engaging students in an exploration of the structure supports their developing understanding of the convention.

MP.8

"Look for and express regularity in repeated reasoning" (NGA Center and CCSSO 2010, p. 8). Another goal of task 2.8 is for students to use their experience with the drawing of tables and repeated examples to generate a general rule for any number of tables. By attending to the repeated calculations, students engage in both the variant (the number that changes as each table is added on) and the constant (the number that stays the same no matter how many tables are present, as long as there is at least one).

Chapter 3
Number and Operations in Base Ten

It is critical that students develop a deep understanding of place value in base ten. Standard U.S. algorithms for whole number and decimal computation—as well as many alternative algorithms such as the partial products, differences, and sums featured in various curricula—are based on manipulations of digits with an understanding of place value. It is helpful for teachers to become familiar with some of the history of the development of our base-ten system, which to us seems so "natural," so they will better understand why learning this system presents at least some students with difficulties.

Our number system, often referred to as the Hindu-Arabic number system, has "three important features . . . (place value, the use of 0 as a place holder, and the use of base 10)" (Barnett 1998, p. 69). Although some of these features were used in earlier number systems, a system that incorporated all three seems to have been developed originally in India, later traveling to the Middle East, and ultimately being introduced to Western Europe during the Middle Ages. Calculating with numbers in this system without the use of an abacus-like counting board was nonetheless not common until the twelfth century. Furthermore, disputes continued in Europe until into the sixteenth century about whether to perform arithmetic operations by writing numbers (employing place value/positional notation) or by using counting rods or an abacus along with the additive system (Roman numerals).

The following sections provide some basic background and explanation for the three defining elements of our number system.

Base ten—Our base-ten number system uses ten digits (0–9) to represent all numbers. The position of the digit within a number is what determines its value. This contrasts with non-positional number systems or additive systems such as Roman numerals. Before positional notation (such as we use in our base-ten system) became common, abacuses and counting rods were used to represent numbers using a concrete positional system of moving beads or rods within columns. It was not until the sixteenth century that calculating on paper instead of by abacus became prevalent.

But why base ten? Many people point to the fact that humans have ten fingers. This may be a good argument, although the Mayans and Babylonians (and other civilizations) were able to develop number systems that used other bases and still functioned well. It seems clear that we use a base-ten system because that was the one that was developed in India and spread to Western Europe. This leaves the question unanswered as to why the Hindu number system was base ten, but whatever causes resulted in the adoption of this system, it is what we use and now seems completely natural.

Place value—Understanding place value requires more than being able to identify place value names (e.g., ones, tens, hundreds, etc.) and identify what number is in a particular place value. Understanding place value also involves understanding that a single digit can have different values concurrently. For example, in the number 2,438, the digit 4 represents the value of 4 hundreds (4 × 100) but can also have the value of 40 tens or 400 ones. This understanding involves multiplicative reasoning. Since multiplicative thinking develops later than additive thinking, it is understandable that knowledge of place value develops over time; it is not unusual for children at the end of grade 2 to still have a fragile understanding of place value. Children in upper elementary grades use place value understandings and properties of operations to perform multi-digit arithmetic that eventually includes decimals.

Zero—There are two different uses of zero: zero as a placeholder and zero as a number in its own right. In addition to using combinations of digits to represent all numbers, our base-ten system (and systems that use other bases, such as the base-2 system used in computer programming) depends on having a number that represents nothing, or zero. The corresponding digit 0 is used as a placeholder within a number, indicating that there is no numeric value to that particular position in the number, while at the same time maintaining the required number of digits for that number so that the other digits fall in their appropriate positions. This ensures, for example, that three hundred five (305) is written differently from thirty-five (35). The first recorded use of zero is by the Babylonians in the third century BCE as part of their sexagesimal (base 60) number system, although the Babylonians did not have a digit for zero but instead left a space indicating nothing was in that place. The Mayans began to use zero as part of their vigesimal (base 20) positional number system a century or so before the documented use of zero in India in the fifth century CE. As indicated above, it is most likely that it was from India through the Islamic countries that in about the twelfth century CE, Western Europe became acquainted with base-ten notation, including the notion of and symbolization for zero.

The concept of zero as a number was slow in being accepted. The very idea of zero was troubling to the ancient Greeks and Romans, who were uncomfortable with the idea of a number (i.e., something) that was nothing. This uneasiness persisted during the Middle Ages in Western Europe, and at times it took the form of religious disputes about the nature and existence of zero. Is it terribly surprising, then, that the use of zero holds such challenges for children?

Teaching and Learning Number and Operations in Base Ten

The Common Core State Standards for Mathematics (CSSSM) indicate that students in kindergarten should work with numbers 11–19, composing and decomposing them along base-ten lines in order to begin to develop an understanding of place value. In grades 1 and 2, students extend their place value understandings and begin to use understandings of place value in addition and subtraction computation. That said, if students arrive at a particular grade (such as grade 3) without a good understanding of a particular standard in the Numbers and Operations in Base Ten domain for previous grades, teachers can address the needs of many of those students by engaging them in the same tasks presented in this volume, but using numbers in a range appropriate to the students' needs.

According to the Common Core State Standards for Mathematics (CCSSM), the learning trajectory for students within the domain of Number and Operations in Base Ten involves a focus in grades 3 and 4 on using place value understandings and properties of operations to perform multi-digit arithmetic; this focus shifts in grade 5 to include performing operations with decimals to hundredths. This movement in grade 5 also includes expanding an understanding of the base-ten place value system, or use of positional notation, from whole numbers to decimal fractions, thus completing engagement with the base-ten system.

There are two main clusters within CCSSM for grades 3–5 that address Number and Operations in Base Ten: Using Place Value and Understanding Place Value. It might seem necessary to understand the base-ten system before being able to use those understandings, but in fact the two develop together. Looking across these two clusters, we have identified four areas that require attention: (*a*) rounding; (*b*) computation using base-ten principles; (*c*) reading, writing, and comparing numbers; and (*d*) understanding place value. The fourth area, understanding place value, is often also at play within each of the first three areas, something we try to note as we present particular tasks below.

As elsewhere in this volume, in this chapter we take an across-the-grades approach to developing tasks for students. At any grade level, there will be students at different places in their understanding of place value in base ten and their ability to manipulate the base-ten system. In addition, this type of organization can be helpful for teachers who work in multi-grade or multi-age contexts.

Table 3.1

Content areas, grade-level standards, and mathematical practice standards met by the tasks in chapter 3

Content Areas	Tasks	Grade 3 Standards	Grade 4 Standards	Grade 5 Standards	Standards for Mathematical Practice
Rounding	3.1	3.NBT.1	4.NBT.3	5.NBT.4	MP.1, MP.2, MP.7
	3.2	3.NBT.1	4.NBT.3	5.NBT.4	
Computation using base-ten principles	3.3	3.NBT.2		5.NBT.7	MP.3, MP.8
	3.4	3.NBT.3		5.NBT.2	
	3.5		4.NBT.4 4.NBT.5	5.NBT.5	
Reading, writing, and comparing numbers	3.6		4.NBT.2	5.NBT.3	MP.6
Understanding how the base-ten system works	3.7		4.NBT.1	5.NBT.1	MP.2, MP.4

Rounding

One method of estimation is called rounding. Rounding a number eliminates one or more of the digits 1–9 from one or more of the positions in the number, and replaces them with 0. When computing with the rounded number, the results are less accurate, but the rounded number is easier to operate on, thus facilitating estimation. While rounding may seem like a purely procedural activity, there is both logic and convention at work when numbers are rounded. Rounding depends on the ability to place a number correctly between two other numbers (e.g., placing 48 between 40 and 50 when rounding to the nearest 10), and ascertaining which is the shorter distance between 48 and the other two numbers, something that requires an understanding of where a number falls in the counting sequence and on a number line. This is further complicated when dealing with numbers having three or more digits since those numbers can be rounded to multiple places. Children need to understand what is meant by rounding to a particular place value, such as the nearest ten, or hundred, or tenth. When rounding 148 to the nearest ten, for example, we are asking whether 148 is closer to 140 or to 150. In a similar way when rounding 148 to the nearest 100 we are asking whether 148 is closer to 100 or 200. This can be confusing to children as they may consider multiple options before deciding on a course of action. Placing the number on a number line may facilitate the process of identifying the distance between the target number and the two decade (multiples of ten) or century (multiples of 100) or millennial (multiples of 1000) numbers under consideration. For example, a number line can be useful in seeing that 148 is closer to 150 than 140 and closer to 100 than 200. In task 3.1, we ask students to place a number on two number lines to facilitate understanding the difference between rounding to 10s and 100s (3.NBT.1). Tasks such as this one support students in developing an understanding that numbers can be placed between many pairs of other numbers depending on the context, and that this is useful when considering rounding.

When we deal with a case such as 45, however, we find that it lies the same distance from both 40 and 50 on a number line. In this case, by convention, the mathematics community has agreed that when rounding 45 to the nearest 10 the result is 50. This is not something that children can determine by observation and application of the logic used in the examples for 148 above; it is something that simply needs to be established as a mathematical convention that is commonly accepted and used. This does not mean that children need only be told this "rule" to memorize. As you will see in task 3.2, there are ways of engaging students in figuring out this convention, thus increasing the possibility of remembering it.

Task 3.1: Where on the Number Line Am I?

Look at the number lines A and B in figure 3.1. What are the similarities and differences between the two number lines? Consider the number 148. Where on number line A would we place 148? Where on number line B? Talk to your partner group about your thinking.

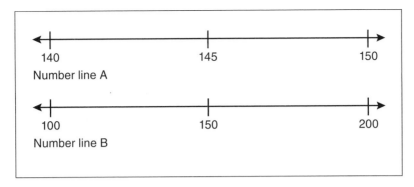

Fig. 3.1. Number lines A and B

Now consider the following numbers: 672, 407, 813, and 387. In your groups, construct two sets of number lines for each number and place that number on both number lines. You will have two number lines for 672, two for 407, two for 813, and two for 387.

Launching the Task—Launch the task by focusing on placing a number on a number line in order to activate previous knowledge about number lines and number placement on those lines. Engage the class in considering a number such as 586. Ask for some examples of numbers that are greater than and less than that number. List those numbers on the board in two columns headed "less than 586" and "greater than 586" as students offer suggestions. Note that students may suggest numbers as low as zero (or possibly lower if they have had some exposure to negative numbers) and as high as 1,000,000 or more. Next choose one of the suggested numbers that is less than 586 and one that is greater. Write the three numbers on the board from least to greatest. Your selection should be strategic so that the range from lowest to highest is at least 100 but not much more to facilitate placing 586 between them. (If it is more comfortable for you to manage, you can ask for suggestions that are multiples of 100 so that you can select 500 and 600 as the comparison numbers to work with, thus assisting students in placing 586 between those two century numbers.) Now ask a student to draw a number line and place a point on the number line for the smallest number. Then ask another student to place a point on the number line for the largest number. Finally engage students in a discussion about where to place 586 on the number line. You may also want to engage students in a discussion about the difficulty of computing with a number like 586 in comparison to a more friendly number, such as 600, which it lies close to on a number line. This type of discussion helps students see the utility of knowing how to round.

Task Exploration—Explain to the students that today they will be placing a number on two different number lines between two different sets of numbers. Read through the task together or have students read it within their groups. As you circulate around the room, you can observe students who may be having a variety of difficulties with the task such as (*a*) constructing number lines with appropriate end points and midpoint, (*b*) placing numbers on the number line accurately, and (*c*) making appropriate rounding decisions. Ask those students to explain their thinking. Note these difficulties so that they can be raised and confronted in the summarizing discussion. Also ask students who seem to be able to accomplish the task more easily to explain their thinking. These students may have a coherent explanation of their decision-making processes that will support the developing understanding of other students.

Summarizing Discussion—Begin the discussion by asking students how they knew which numbers to choose for endpoints and midpoints on the various number lines. Ask them how they determined where to place the target number in reference to the other three points. Once students are comfortable considering placing numbers between decade and century numbers, they are ready to articulate the system we use to round numbers. Explain to students (if they are not already familiar with the terminology) that we use the term "rounding" to describe the decisions they have been making with regard to which endpoint the target number is closer to. Engage students in a conversation using the following questions:

- How did you decide where to place your target numbers when there is a distance of 10 between endpoints on the number line?

- How did you decide where to place your target numbers when there is a distance of 100 between endpoints on the number line?

Explain to students that in the first case we say that we are "rounding to the nearest 10," and in the second case, "rounding to the nearest 100." Continue the discussion with the following question:

- If you had to explain to people who did not know about how to round numbers, how would you go about explaining to them how to do it?

Adapting for Grades 4 and 5—This task can be extended to address the grade 4 standard on rounding multi-digit numbers to any place (4.NBT.3) and the grade 5 standard on rounding decimals to any place (5.NBT.4). To explore rounding a large multi-digit number like 12,327, for example, you could construct number lines with points (*a*) 12,320 and 12,330, (*b*) 12,300 and 12,400, and (*c*) 12,000 and 13,000 and examine placing 12,327 when rounding to tens, hundreds, and thousands, respectively. Other numbers that you determine might be particularly useful for your students to explore can be used. In the same way, to examine scenarios for rounding decimals such as 0.726, number lines with points (*a*) 0.700 and 0.800 and (*b*) 0.720 and 0.730 could be constructed to examine placing 0.726 in order to facilitate decision making for rounding to tenths or hundredths, respectively.

Task 3.2: What's My Rule?

What happens when we try to round a number that lies on the midpoint between two decade or century numbers? Look at the first two columns of table 3.2. To arrive at the number in the "Out #1" column, the numbers have been rounded to the nearest ten. What rule do you think has been used there? When you think you have figured this out, look at the final two columns. In this case, to arrive at the number in the "Out #2" column, the numbers were rounded to the nearest 100. What rule do you think was used in this case? Discuss your ideas with your group and be prepared to share your thinking with the entire class. (*Note:* The table can be written on the board or given to students along with the problem as a handout.)

Table 3.2
Results of rounding

In	Out #1	In	Out #2
148	150	148	100
562	560	562	600
235	240	235	200
605	610	605	600
458	460	458	500
485	490	485	500
		150	200

Launching the Task—One way to launch the task would be to engage students in stipulating the familiar rule you used to determine the "out" number in the In and Out Box in table 3.3. Provide students with a copy of table 3.3 or put the chart on the board. Students in grade 3 and above will generally easily see that the value in the "out" box is one more than the value in the "in" box and be able to stipulate that the rule was to add one. Tell students that you are now going to use some of these same numbers and some new numbers in the "in" box, and you will then apply first one new rule and then a second new rule to them.

Table 3.3
In and Out Box

In	Out
148	149
562	563
235	236
605	606

Task Exploration—As you circulate around the room while students are working on task 3.2, you will notice which students are easily able to determine the rule for rounding in the special case when the target digit is 5. If you see that some students are having a more difficult time, you can suggest that constructing a number line as they did in task 3.1 might assist them. This will allow you to observe whether some students might still be having difficulty determining which multiples of 10 or 100 to use as endpoints of their number lines and if students know the midpoints for these number lines. If students are not able to do that, you may need to return to task 3.1 (if not today, then at a different time), choosing different numbers and engaging in discussion about placing numbers between appropriate multiples of 10 or 100 for the purposes of facilitating rounding. In fact, you can engage students in task 3.1 using exclusively values that would place the target number on the midpoint, thus providing a graphic example of rounding up when the target digit is 5 (and any lower place values are zero).

Summarizing Discussion—As in task 3.1, useful questions for engaging students include the following:

- How did you decide what the rule was in the first case? In the second case?
- How would you explain this to a student who was unfamiliar with these special cases of rounding?

It is important that students grasp the notion that the distance on the number line from 0–5 is equal to the distance from 5–10 and that mathematicians have made a decision that when rounding in this case we round up.

STANDARDS *for Mathematical Practice—Tasks 3.1 and 3.2*

MP.1

The first Standard for Mathematical Practice states, "Make sense of problems and persevere in solving them" (National Governors Association Center for Best Practices and Council of Chief State School Officers [NGA Center and CCSSO] 2010, p. 6). This standard in particular is highly visible across all parts of the three-part lesson format and applies to all problem-solving lessons. For that reason, we will discuss it briefly here in a general way and not raise it again in relation to other tasks within this chapter. Within the *launch* portion of the lesson, teachers can support students in understanding the task and finding an entry point they will be comfortable using. In this way students become accustomed to interrogating the meaning of the task and deciding on an approach to solving. They are then ultimately able to do this independently. During the *exploration* portion of the lesson, teachers can support students in "monitor[ing] and evaluat[ing] their progress" (NGA Center and CCSSO 2010, p. 6), as well as attempting other approaches should the original choice of solution path prove ineffective. This can be done through careful questioning on the part of the teacher during the *exploration*. During the *discussion* portion of the lesson, the teacher provides an opportunity to "understand the approaches of others to solving complex problems and identify correspondences between different approaches" (NGA Center and CCSSO 2010, p. 6) as she scaffolds and facilitates discussion of various solutions to the task at hand.

MP.2

"Reason abstractly and quantitatively" (NGA Center and CCSSO 2010, p. 6). Tasks 3.1 and 3.2 provide students with an opportunity to reason about the mathematics, moving from using a visual number line model to reasoning about placement of numbers in relation to other numbers, to extrapolating a "rule" that can be applied in the absence of that number line. It is important to note that while both task 3.1 and task 3.2 are bare number problems having no real-world or approximate real-world context within which the mathematics is embedded, they also qualify as problem-solving tasks. As we mentioned in the introductory chapter, bare number problems can also involve problem solving. Any task in which the mathematics is problematized for the students, as it is in these two tasks, qualifies as a problem-solving task. This problematizing involves engaging students with reasoning about the tasks and not simply following a rule or procedure given by the teacher.

MP.7

"Look for and make use of structure" (NGA Center and CCSSO 2010, p. 8). The two tasks in the section provide students with an opportunity to examine structural elements of our base-ten number system, such as that any three-digit number can be located between two multiples of 100 (from 100–1000). Students can then notice patterns in the distances between the target number and those multiples of 100. In this way, rounding becomes a sense-making activity instead of one simply reliant on following what may seem like arbitrary rules passed down by the teacher or the textbook.

Computation Using Base-Ten Principles

In order to be successful with standard U.S. algorithms, students need to be able to decompose numbers along base-ten lines. In grades 3 and 4, students develop competence in applying place value properties to multi-digit computation with whole numbers. In grade 5, competence in applying place value properties in computation is extended to decimal numbers to hundredths. In the tasks that follow, we present games and activities that address not simply developing procedural fluency with computation but also analysis of computation and engagement with computation that enhance the understanding of the base-ten system.

Adding fluently within 1000 (3.NBT.2) can be supported by a game such as the one in task 3.3, in which students manipulate cards with digits 0–9 to make two three-digit numbers which when added have a sum as close to 1000 as possible. This game (which is modeled after one in the curriculum *Investigations in Number, Data, and Space*) not only supports students in achieving fluency in addition within 1000 but also in decision making about how to use each digit in constructing the number. Considering, for example, whether the digit 3 should be used as a hundreds digit, a tens digit, or a ones digit engages students in grappling with one of the essential issues of place value.

Multiplication is a concept that students begin to work with in grade 2 (2.OA.3 and 2.OA.4), and various clusters of standards within the Operation and Algebraic Thinking domain at grade 3 are largely focused on aspects of developing multiplication (and division) concepts and skills. As students move through the grades 3–5 grade band, the Common Core State Standards indicate that they should develop ever more sophisticated computational skills in multiplication (and division), increasing their knowledge from multi-digit whole number computation in grade 4 to include computation of decimals to the hundredths in grade 5. Multiplying a single-digit number by a multiple of ten (3.NBT.3), as explored in task 3.4, is a useful step to take to provide experiences that support movement to multiplying multi-digit numbers and is an important standard for grade 3.

Although the standards for grade 4 (4.NBT.4 and 4.NBT.5) and grade 5 (5.NBT.5) regarding computation of multi-digit numbers may read rather procedurally, these computations can be problematized for students in order to enhance their understanding of how place value is related to computation. Further skill development in addition and multiplication can come from comparing standard and nonstandard algorithms in a way that emphasizes the role of place value in the standard U. S. algorithm, as provided by task 3.5.

Task 3.3: Target 1000

Today we are going to be playing a game called "Target 1000." Students will work in pairs, or in groups of three or four. The objective of the game is to make two three-digit numbers that add to a sum that is as close to 1000 as possible. Each group will use a deck of cards with the digits 0–9. Deal out eight cards to each person. Your cards can be placed faceup in front you. There is no advantage to hiding your cards from your group. From these eight cards, each person uses six of the cards to make two three-digit numbers. Use your eight cards to try different combinations of digits to construct the two numbers so that the sum of them is as close to 1000 as possible. For example, if you were dealt the cards in figure 3.2, you might make the two three-digit numbers, seen in figure 3.3, that add up to 1002, just two more than 1000.

Fig. 3.2. Possible eight cards dealt to a student

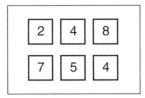

Fig. 3.3. Possible three-digit numbers made from dealt cards

When each person in the group has constructed his or her numbers, and determined the sum and its difference from 1000, share your thinking on how you decided which digits to use. Help each other see whether there are other combinations that would have resulted in a sum closer to 1000.

Launching the Task—For this task, you can use commercially produced sets of number cards, or make your own out of construction paper that you laminate for durability. It is also possible to use commercial playing cards, substituting the ace for the digit 1 and one of the face cards for the digit 0, but this may be confusing to some students. The first time you play this game in class, the launch will have to include a demonstration of how to play the game. You might consider teaching it to a couple students before the whole class begins to work with the game so that those students can be the ones to demonstrate and explain (or help you demonstrate and explain) the rules. When the game is played subsequently, it can be launched with a review of the rules and a discussion about what was challenging or fun about playing the game. This may include issues involving relationships among the students that arose during game play as well as mathematical issues.

You can make this a more competitive game by instructing the students to record the distance of their sum from 1000 and compare who has the lowest "score" after several rounds, but we think cooperative game playing serves more students.

Task Exploration—Students will engage in the game during the task exploration. The teacher can circulate among the groups ensuring that everyone understands how to play. The teacher can use the time to assess which students are comfortable and confident in their play and which ones are more tentative or are having difficulty in constructing the most successful combinations. Teachers might ask groups whether there are other combinations that could produce the same or a better result. In the example in figure 3.3, for instance, the teacher might ask whether 258 and 744 would produce the same or a different result and why. Thinking about this and explaining it also engages students in considering place value.

Summarizing Discussion—The discussion can revolve around the strategies that students found effective in constructing their numbers. Students' initial strategy is often to choose two digits to place in the hundreds place in their numbers whose sum is ten, thinking that this will insure that they get to 1000. Since this gives them a sum of 1000 before adding in any tens or ones, their sum is often much larger than 1000. From these experiences some students develop a strategy that involves choosing digits for the hundreds place that sum to 9, leaving room between 900 and 1000 for digits in the tens and ones. Students may use a variety of strategies, however, and the discussion can be a lively one.

Adapting for Grade 5—This task could also be adapted to address the grade 5 standard 5.NBT.7, computing with decimals. Decimal point cards could be given to each student and students could be dealt six cards from which they could choose four cards to construct two two-digit decimals (decimals in the hundredths) so that when added, they produced a sum close to 1.0.

Task 3.4: Buying Tickets at the School Fair

Tickets for activities at the school fair are sold in packs of ten. How many tickets will you need if each member of your family is going to use 10 tickets? 20 tickets? 30 tickets? 40 tickets? 50 tickets? What if every family member uses 60 tickets? 70 tickets? 80 tickets? 90 tickets? Record your thinking in table 3.4.

Table 3.4
Number of tickets my family needs

# of people in my family	# of tickets per person	# of tickets my family needs
	10 tickets	
	20 tickets	
	30 tickets	
	40 tickets	
	50 tickets	
	60 tickets	
	70 tickets	
	80 tickets	
	90 tickets	

Launching the Task—Engage students in a discussion of fairs or carnivals they have attended. Students may have had experience with county or state fairs, urban street fairs, or traveling carnivals. Most students have probably been to a school fair, either at their own school or at the schools of their siblings, cousins, or friends. Ask students what their favorite events were at the fairs or carnivals they attended. If your school has a yearly school carnival or fair, lead students in a discussion of their experiences at that event. Next ask students how the events they attended were paid for. Most fairs and carnivals run on a ticket economy, with attendees buying tickets and using those tickets to access rides and activities. Explain to students that at one particular school fair, tickets are only sold in packs of ten. Their job in this activity will be to figure out how many tickets their family will use, depending on the number of tickets that each family member is allowed. Tell them that when they are finished with the task, they should discuss their results with others in their group and be prepared to share their thinking with the whole class.

Task Exploration—Hand out a sheet that has a reproduction of table 3.4. Since the task is asking students about the number of tickets necessary for their own family, responses will differ. This can provide good information for the summarizing discussion. As you circulate, you can observe and ask students how they are determining the number of tickets their families will need. You may see students skip counting or employing repeated addition. If you have students who could benefit from using the tens sticks from base-ten blocks to model the numbers of tickets, you can make those available, although using these manipulatives can be unwieldy with large numbers.

Summarizing Discussion—Begin the discussion by collecting information on the number of tickets per person needed for the families of a variety of students. Record this information using blank charts similar to the one in table 3.5. (The numbers in the charts in table 3.5 are provided as examples.) It is recommended that you use one "10 tickets per person" chart, along with tables for two or three other multiples of 10. Elicit from students the patterns they notice first when each family member receives 10 tickets. Students will probably notice that the number of people in the family and the number of tickets needed differ only in that the number of tickets needed has a zero at the end of the number. Likewise, in the charts recording a multiple of 10 tickets per family member, students are likely to notice a pattern such as that $4 \times 40 = 160$ and $4 \times 4 = 16$. These observations can help children who achieved their results by skip counting or repeated addition to see that they can use known multiplication facts to arrive at a solution through a more efficient solution path.

Table 3.5
Number of tickets needed per family

10 tickets per person		40 tickets per person	
# of people in my family	# of tickets my family needs	# of people in my family	# of tickets my family needs
4	40	4	160
7	70	7	280

Adapting for Grade 5—To address standard 5.NBT.2, students can be engaged in a discussion of what the results would be if each person in a family received 100 or even the improbable quantity of 1,000 tickets. In this way, students would be positioned to consider the effect of multiplying a number by a power of 10. This task may also address standards in the Operations and Algebraic Thinking domain, such as 3.OA.8 and 4.OA.3, by writing expressions using a letter or a box to stand for the unknown value.

Task 3.5: Comparing Algorithms for Addition

Look at the examples of addition methods in figure 3.4. What do you notice? With your group, discuss the differences and similarities among the methods. Write down the things you notice that are similar and those that are different. When you finish this, use each of these methods to calculate the sum of 536,238 + 281,791. You can work with a partner to do this. Be prepared to share your thinking on both parts of this problem with the whole class.

Method A

30,000	+2000	+500	+40	9	
+10,000	+4000	+600	+30	6	
40,000	+6000	+1100	+70	+15	= 47,185

Method B

3	2,	5	4	9
+1	4,	6	3	6
			1	5
			7	0
	1	1	0	0
	6	0	0	0
4	0	0	0	0
4	7,	1	8	5

Method C

	1		1		
3	2,	5	4	9
+1	4,	6	3	6
4	7,	1	8	5

Fig. 3.4. Methods for calculating that 32,549 + 14,636 = 47,185

Launching the Task—Place an addition problem such as 49 + 24 on the board, and ask students to do the addition mentally. After giving students time to think, ask them what result they got. A likely result will be the correct answer of 73. Ask a number of students how they arrived at their answers. Some may say that they thought of 49 as 50 and then added 24 to arrive at 74; they then subtracted 1 to compensate for having added 1 to 49. Others may say that they added 40 and 20 and got 60 and then added 9 and 4 and got 13; they then added 60 and 13 to arrive at 73. Validate for students that there are a variety of different ways in which computation, both mental and using paper and pencil, can be accomplished. Explain to them that today they are going to work in groups to consider three different methods that other students (and perhaps they themselves) have used to add large numbers. Their job during the task exploration will be to compare these methods and then use each of them to solve the addition problem 536,238 + 281,791. If you think it would be helpful to your students, you could have grid paper available for students to use in working on the addition problem.

Task Exploration—List on the board the examples of methods used to compute the problem 32,549 + 14,636 = 47,185 as seen in figure 3.4. As you circulate around the room, discuss the various similarities and differences that students are noticing. Differences may include such things as that in method A there are addition signs between the numbers on the lowest line and that in method B there are many sub or partial sums (although students may not call them this) shown in comparison to method C, which has only one number below the line. Students may also notice that method C is the only method where there are "small number ones" written above the first addend. Similarities may include that the final sums are the same in all three problems. Students may also notice that the partial products in method A also appear in method B but are absent in method C. As students move on to working on calculating the sum of 536,238 + 281,791 using the three methods presented in figure 3.4, notice which students are able to manage the three algorithms easily and which ones are having more difficulty.

Although the example used in this task is comparison of algorithms for addition, this same idea can be used to compare algorithms for any of the four basic operations and in this way address standards in both grades 4 and 5.

Summarizing Discussion—Begin by asking students to share what they noticed in comparing the three methods of addition shown in figure 3.4. Students may raise some of the points mentioned above. Ask students which method they found to be the most comfortable to use and why. This may produce a variety of answers and reasons. Tell students that method C (the standard U.S. algorithm) is a method that many people in the United States use. Ask them what they see as some of the advantages of this method over the other two. Someone is likely to point out that you waste less paper and pencil lead when using that method, as it takes up less space on the page and is shorter to write. In fact, its succinctness is one of the reasons that this algorithm is so widely used in the U.S. as well as in other countries. It is important to note that although our goal is to support children in developing facility with the standard U.S. algorithm (method C), we do not want this to happen at the expense of understanding or accuracy. Students may need many opportunities with computing with a method of their choosing before they are ready to adopt the standard U. S. algorithm.

STANDARDS *for Mathematical Practice—Tasks 3.3 through 3.5*

MP.3

"Construct viable arguments and critique the reasoning of others" (NGA Center and CCSSO 2010, p. 6) is the third Standard for Mathematical Practice. In a task such as task 3.3, students have the opportunity to argue why they have chosen to use particular digits in each place value when constructing their numbers. Furthermore, they have the opportunity to listen to the arguments of their peers as to the reasons for their choices. During this task, students address this standard in both the task exploration and summarizing discussion portions of the lesson. If students have no opportunity, such as the one this task provides, to listen and respond to the reasoning of other students, it is unlikely that they will be able to meet this standard. For teachers, it is important to note that being able to engage in an academic discussion is a learned skill, and building a culture of discourse and communication in the classroom will be key in ensuring that all students have the necessary skills to participate in discussion.

MP.8

"Look for and express regularity in repeated reasoning" (NGA Center and CCSSO 2010, p. 8). Task 3.4 provides an opportunity for students to explore and express regularity and repetition. When multiplying a number by a power of ten, for example, patterns emerge such as that the number of zeros in the final place values of the product equal the number of zeros in the multiple of ten being used as a factor. Although we do not want to teach something like this as a "rule" (i.e., when multiplying by a power of ten you append the number of zeros that are in the multiple of ten to the other factor), it is useful for students to notice this regularity that happens.

Comparing algorithms also gives students an opportunity to see regularity in how various methods notate partial sums (in the case of task 3.5). In comparing computation methods, students see that partial sums are represented in all cases. They can extend that thinking to consider that any given algorithm will represent all partial sums in some way all of the time.

Reading, Writing, and Comparing Numbers

In grade 4, students extend understandings they had begun to develop in grade 2 for comparing numbers using the symbols =, <, and >. Whereas in grade 2 they were comparing three-digit numbers, in grade 4 they extend this to comparisons of larger multi-digit whole numbers (4.NBT.2). In grade 5, they further expand comparing numbers to decimals in the thousandths, along with reading and writing those numbers using numerals, number names, and expanded form (5.NBT.3). Number comparisons are more motivating and meaningful for students if they use contexts that students find interesting or familiar. Comparing populations of cities, states, or countries can provide motivation for examining and comparing large numbers. For students who live in a major metropolitan area, comparisons of other cities in the U.S. or the world might work well. For students who live in smaller rural towns, comparisons of the population of their state with that of other states in the U.S. can provide a context to engage with larger numbers (see task 3.6). For immigrant students, comparing the population of the U.S. with other countries can be fruitful. With the quantity of data easily available on the Internet, many other contexts besides population could be used, such as the number of gallons of water used by people in various states or countries per month or per year. A context that is meaningful to your students is what will work best.

Task 3.6: Which State Is Bigger?

Did you ever wonder which U.S. state has the largest population? Did you ever wonder how the population of [include the name of your state] compares to that of other states? Work in your group to compare states in terms of their population. Choose two states and write them on your recording sheet (see table 3.6). Through discussion in your group, decide which state you believe has the larger population and indicate that on your recording sheet as well. Then choose another two states (one of the states can be the same as one of your first choices) and compare those two. Do this as many times as you have time for.

Table 3.6
Comparison of states

Name of state	Population	Is bigger/smaller than	Name of state	Population

Launching the Task—To launch this task, engage your class in a discussion of which states they believe have the largest and the smallest populations. Have a U.S. map or a list of U.S. states available to help students recall the names of states. As your class offers suggestions, list them on the board. Because students may know that New York, Los Angeles, and Chicago are large U.S. cities, they may predict that New York, California, and Illinois are states with large populations. Predicting states with small populations may be more difficult and may result in a variety of suggestions. Students also might have little idea of the ranking of states by population and simply guess. Whatever suggestions your class offers will not affect their engagement with the task. After you have listed a number of states on the board, ask students to guess the population of one or two. As students offer suggestions, write those numbers next to the particular state. This is one way that students can be engaged with seeing the correct numerical representation, written by the teacher, of their verbal expression of the number name. Next give your class a handout that lists the U.S. states and their populations. Make sure that the list is large enough for students to be able to see the numbers easily. Have students highlight or mark in some way those states that they have listed on the board. Explain to them that they are going to work in groups to compare the populations of some pairs of those states. Before students begin to work on the task, engage the entire class in a discussion of any surprises they see when examining the populations of the various states. Ask them such questions as:

- What were you thinking when you predicted the population of [name of a particular state]?
- On what were you basing your opinion?

This discussion can help anchor students' own ideas to the task at hand.

Task Exploration—Provide students with a sheet on which to record their comparisons. The sheet should contain a series of fill-in-the-blank sections that look something like table 3.6. Groups can then work at comparing two states and listing the results. At this point it is not important for students to use < and > symbols, although it is fine if they do. Some students may be competent in using them while others may still find them confusing. During the task exploration, the important idea for students to grapple with is comparison of numbers. The notation for greater than and less than can be discussed during the summarizing discussion.

As you circulate around the room during the task exploration you will see who in your class has enough understanding (either procedural or conceptual) of place value to make these comparisons accurately. You can see which students are struggling to accomplish the task accurately, noting what their misconceptions might be in order to address them during the summarizing discussion. Comparing numbers can be difficult for many elementary students. When students attend to individual digits, they may think, for example, that 911 is greater than 1111 since 911 contains the digit 9 in the leading position and 1111 begins with the digit 1.

Summarizing Discussion—For the summarizing discussion, have a blank table similar to the one in table 3.6 on the board. Ask groups to volunteer data for you to enter on the table, or have students come forward and enter states and populations. Each time the populations of two states are compared, ask students whether they agree with the thinking of the group suggesting the data. If students challenge erroneous suggestions by another group, ask that group whether they would like to revise their thinking. These types of discussions provide opportunities for students to consider emerging ideas of number comparisons and revise their thinking based on feedback from their peers. Students may bring erroneous ideas to comparing numbers, as indicated above. The teacher should note these ideas while circulating during the task exploration so that she can ensure that they are brought into the summarizing discussion and confronted. It is important that the idea of comparing digits in successive place values is raised during the summarizing discussion. If students are not clear about this being the basis of their decision making when making comparisons, the teacher should be sure to introduce this idea. This might be done by placing the populations of two states (we will continue with the New York and California examples) one above the other for easy comparison as in table 3.7.

Table 3.7
Comparison of the populations of California and New York

California	37,691,912
New York	19,645,197

While recording data on the chart, you can use the greater (>) and less than (<) symbols instead of the larger/smaller language some students may have used during the task exploration. After you have entered a number of comparisons on the table, you can remind the class that in making comparisons between numbers, mathematicians use the < and > symbols. Some useful questions are:

- Can someone explain why in some cases the symbol is oriented in one direction and in other cases it is oriented in the other direction?

- Does the order in which the numbers are listed impact the symbol, and if so how?

During this discussion, students who have mastered the use of the < and > symbols can offer insights that may help their peers who have a more fragile understanding. As in previous tasks, it may be helpful to have students articulate how they would explain these symbols and their use to someone who was unfamiliar with them.

Adapting for Grade 5—This task can be adapted for grade 5 by using baseball batting averages (statistics available from www.baseball-almanac.com/hitting/hibavg1.shtml) instead of population. The use of these data can be particularly motivating for students who follow baseball or are involved with other sports, as many students, boys and girls alike, do. They may bring to the problem knowledge that they have of which players have the highest batting averages currently or historically. This positions them to understand comparing decimals to the thousandths more generally, in relation to this specific knowledge they possess. It also positions those students as experts who during the task exploration and summarizing discussion can support other students in understanding comparisons of decimals. Although batting averages almost always involve decimals of 0.366 and lower, they do provide extensive opportunities for comparison of the hundredths and thousandths place values, something that students in grade 5 have had less opportunity to do. Other sports statistics can be used to engage with decimal values closer to one. Free throw statistics for NBA basketball players, for example, may range from 0.903 to 0.497 (http://www.basketball-reference.com/leaders/ft_pct_career.html).

STANDARDS *for Mathematical Practice—Task 3.6*

MP.6

The sixth Standard for Mathematical Practice is *"Attend to precision"* (NGA Center and CCSSO 2010, p. 7). To compare large numbers, students must attend precisely to place values in numbers as well as to the precise use of the greater than (>) and less than (<) symbols. The seemingly arbitrary nature of these similar symbols with their dual directionality can make it difficult for students to use precisely. Tasks such as task 3.6 support them in developing (or cementing) understanding of these important mathematical symbols.

Understanding How the Base-Ten System Works

While the understanding of multi-digit place value is developing throughout grades 3 and 4, a solid understanding of place value as it applies to multi-digit numbers should develop by the end of grade 4 (4.NBT.1), and by the end of grade 5 students should have a solid understanding of our base-ten place value system as it applies to all whole numbers and decimals (5.NBT.1, 5.NBT.2). Understanding the base-ten system involves extended work and thinking on the part of children. Working with such manipulatives as base-ten blocks and MultiLink cubes to model grouping of one, ten, and one hundred is useful, but this becomes awkward when working with larger numbers. In this case, a concrete and imaginable context can support students in moving from working with manipulatives to working more consistently with written notation and eventually algorithms both invented and standard. In task 3.7, students are engaged in packaging stickers in groups of 10s, 100s, 1000s, and 10,000s, and in the process they develop an understanding that in a multi-digit number the value of each digit is 10 times the value of the digit to its right and $1/10$ the value of the digit to its left.

Task 3.7: Selling Stickers

Ms. Rivera's class is making and selling stickers as a class project. They will sell stickers packaged in a variety of ways:

a. Single loose stickers

b. Small plastic bags of 10 stickers

c. Packs of 10 small plastic bags

d. Envelopes of 10 packs

e. Boxes of 10 envelopes

Ms. Rivera's class keeps track of their sticker inventory on a sheet like the one shown in table 3.8.

Table 3.8
Inventory recording sheet

Total # of stickers	# of boxes	# of envelopes	# of packs	# of small plastic bags	# of single loose stickers

Today you are going to work with your group to explore the ways in which the stickers that Ms. Rivera's class has in inventory might be distributed within the various types of packaging they use. Be prepared to share your thinking with the whole class.

Launching the Task—One way to launch the task would be to engage students in a discussion of the way they think goods are packaged when they arrive at retail stores. While shopping with adults in their lives and seeing food being unpacked onto grocery store shelves, they may have had experience with seeing, for example, cans of soft drinks packaged in 6-packs and those 6-packs in turn packaged in boxes of 24. This can provide a fruitful lead into packaging stickers.

Since by grades 4 and 5 many students are familiar with Roman numerals (an additive rather than a place value or positional number system), having seen them used as dates in various contexts, another way to launch the task would be to engage students in a lively discussion of what they see (or not) as the benefits of our base-ten place value system in comparison to Roman numerals. Such a discussion which might pique students' interest in how the base-ten number system works, and pave the way for fruitful engagement with task 3.7.

Task Exploration—Provide each student, or each pair of students, with two or three file cards on which you have written a number of stickers, as well as a handout (see table 3.8) on which to record all the different combinations of packaged stickers. As a way to make this experience more concrete, teachers could engage their classes in decorating actual stickers for sale in the school. Small dot or rectangular stickers are available fairly inexpensively from stationery stores.

Encourage the students to find a number of different ways their stickers (imagined or real) could be packaged. The task can be differentiated for learners with differing levels of understanding of place value by providing them with smaller or larger numbers to work with. If you feel your entire class would benefit from working on this task with smaller numbers, you can eliminate the boxes and/or envelopes columns and examine numbers only in the thousands or hundreds. This is one way to adapt the task for grade 3 as well. There is no explicit standard for grade 3 in CCSSM that falls under this category of place value understanding, but students in grade 3 might benefit from the examination of the place value system this task offers.

Students work to determine how the stickers might be packaged, consulting with group members. As students find multiple ways of organizing the stickers, some of these ways will not fall along base-ten lines. For example, a student who was given the number 2342 may say that number of stickers could be packaged as in table 3.9:

Table 3.9
Possible packaging of 2342 stickers

Total # of stickers	# of boxes	# of envelopes	# of packs	# of small plastic bags	# of single loose stickers
2342		2	3	4	2
		1	13	3	12
		1	13	2	22

This is just the kind of information you want from students so that you have it available for the summarizing discussion. Because of their past experiences with putting numbers into columns labeled ones, tens, hundreds, and so forth, some students may be hesitant to think about ways to organize stickers that do not fall along base-ten lines. You can encourage them to expand their thinking by asking such questions as:

- What if one of those plastic bags was emptied? How many plastic bags and single loose stickers would there be then?
- What if one of the envelopes was emptied? How many envelopes and packs of stickers would there be then?

This engagement with thinking about one organization of stickers (packs for example) as containing 10 of the next smaller unit (small plastic bags in this case) supports them in developing the understanding that in any multi-digit number, a digit in one place represents 10 times the digit to its right and $\frac{1}{10}$ of the digit to its left (4.NBT.1 and 5.NBT.1).

Summarizing Discussion—Bring students together to discuss their results. Choose students who have more than one result for a given number such as in table 3.9. Ask students what they notice about the results. If necessary, you can probe with questions such as the ones listed above for the task exploration. Some students may notice that when the stickers are organized along base-ten lines (i.e., with no more than 9 stickers in any given category), the resulting number is the same as the number they were initially given.

- Ask students to explain why they think that is.
- Ask students whether it would ever be possible (in the example of 2342) to have 8 packs of stickers.

Grappling with questions such as this one supports students in seeing that breaking up envelopes will only increase packs by 10 and combining packs will only reduce packs by 10 since 10 packs are needed to make an envelope.

STANDARDS *for Mathematical Practice—Task 3.7*

MP.2

"Reason abstractly and quantitatively" (NGA Center and CCSSO 2010, p. 6). Task 3.7 gives students an opportunity to make sense of the quantity of stickers in relation to the various ways stickers could be packaged. They have the opportunity to see, for example, that having three small plastic bags of stickers is the same as having 30 stickers. These understandings can then be extended to the base-ten number system more generally, where the digit 3 in the tens place means three groups of 10 and at the same time 30.

MP.4

"Model with mathematics" (NGA Center and CCSSO 2010, p. 6). This task also offers an opportunity to model quantities of stickers using a packaging system that mirrors our base-ten system. Working with large quantities in this way provides students with an understandable context for thinking about groupings of ten, which is the basis of the base-ten system.

Conclusion

The base-ten system took considerable time to develop and become an accepted system for writing numbers and using in computation. It is therefore not difficult to see why developing a solid understanding of it requires time and engagement, with many and varied activities and much discussion on the part of students. The tasks in this chapter are offered to assist teachers in their endeavors to engage students with this complex numeric system that we have come to see as so "natural."

Chapter 4
Number and Operations— Fractions

The word *fraction* has its roots in Latin, and it means "to break." Ancient Egyptians used fractions in their everyday lives and started writing them as early as 1800 BCE, but the way they wrote fractions was very different from how we do it today. The way we currently write fractions became popular in the seventeenth century in Europe. To provide students with a big picture about the relevance of fractions, many interesting questions could be posed. For example, what is a fraction? How long have people been using fractions? Why did people start using fractions? Why or when can using fractions be helpful in our lives today? Are fractions always represented in the same way? What are some different ways to represent fractions?

From an instructional perspective, it is important that students be given the opportunity to understand that a fraction is only one type of rational number. Rational numbers also include integers and terminal or repeating decimals. Fractions are distinguished from other rational numbers by representing both the part (i.e., the numerator) and the whole (i.e., the denominator). While other types of rational numbers are not necessarily fractions, they may be represented as fractions (e.g., representing the integer 5 as $^{10}/_2$, or 0.25 as $^1/_4$). Further, in many elementary textbooks, fractions are heavily represented as a part-whole construct with students having to identify the shaded parts of wholes.

In this chapter, we draw upon a problem-solving approach integrated with the use of visual models to help students discover connections between the various aspects of fractions such as whole and unit fractions, equivalent fractions, and the relationships among the operations of addition, subtraction, multiplication, and division in the context of fractions.

Each grade level of the Common Core State Standards for Mathematics (CCSSM) for grades 3–5 has its own set of standards clustered or grouped together to facilitate mathematical connections. One approach to teaching fractions would be to stick to specific grade levels and find tasks that address the clusters and standards *within* grade level. In this chapter, as elsewhere in the book, we take an *across*-grade-levels perspective, with the understanding that at any specific grade level some students will be at different places in their understanding of fractions. Such an organization can be a support for teachers at a specific grade level in differentiating instruction for their students. This across-grade-level organization can also be very helpful for teachers who are in multi-age or multi-grade contexts.

The appendix provides a big picture of the progression of the Common Core Standards from kindergarten to grade 5. Fractions are not introduced until grade 3. The bulk of fraction concepts is expected to be mastered in grades 3–5. Multiplication and division of fractions and problems involving fractions and decimals are introduced in this grade band but are not expected to be mastered until middle school. The Common Core Standards indicate that decimals and the relationship between fractions and decimal notation be introduced in grade 4 (i.e., 4.NF.5–7). The main connection that students need to make between decimal fractions and decimal notation in grades 4–5 is that decimal notation is a way of representing fractions based on place value when the denominator of the fraction is ten or a multiple of ten ($0.1 = \frac{1}{10}$, $0.01 = \frac{1}{100}$, etc.). Such manipulatives as base-ten blocks, drawings, and other visual representations can be used to help students make connections and comparisons between decimal fractions written in fraction form and those written with decimal notation, as well as between two fractions written with decimal notation. Although decimal notation is an important representation of this special class of fractions, in this chapter we do not present problems for which students would need to use decimal notation.

In organizing the standards across grade levels, we identify five distinct areas that need attention when teaching fractions. These five areas include: (1) unit fractions, (2) equivalent fractions, (3) adding and subtracting fractions with both like and unlike denominators, (4) developing an understanding of multiplying fractions (whole number and fraction, as well as fraction and fraction), and (5) developing a beginning understanding of division of fractions limited to unit fractions—that is, dividing whole numbers with unit fractions (e.g., $3 \div \frac{1}{2}$) and unit fractions with whole numbers (e.g., $\frac{1}{2} \div 3$). What follows are problem-solving tasks to support development in understanding and working with unit fractions (tasks 4.1 and 4.2), equivalent fractions (task 4.3), adding and subtracting fractions (tasks 4.4 and 4.5), developing an understanding of multiplying fractions (tasks 4.6, 4.7, and 4.8), and developing a beginning understanding of division of fractions (tasks 4.9 and 4.10). Table 4.1 shows each of these areas together with the relevant tasks and targeted standards. Note that while particular standards are targets, tasks may be extended in different ways to address other standards in the Number and Operations—Fractions domain.

Table 4.1

Content areas, grade-level standards, and mathematical practice standards met by the tasks in chapter 4

Content Areas	Tasks	Grade 3 Standards	Grade 4 Standards	Grade 5 Standards	Standards for Mathematical Practice
Unit fractions	4.1	3.NF.1	4.NF.1		MP.6, MP.7
	4.2	3.NF.1 3.NF.2 3.NF.3d	4.NF.2		
Fraction equivalence	4.3	3.NF.3 3.NF.3b 3.G.2	4.NF.1	5.NF.1 5.NF.2	MP.1, MP.3, MP.6

Table 4.1 Continued

Content Areas	Tasks	Grade 3 Standards	Grade 4 Standards	Grade 5 Standards	Standards for Mathematical Practice
Adding and subtracting fractions	4.4		4.NF.3	5.NF.1 5.NF.2	MP.7
	4.5		4.NF.4	5.NF.4 5.NF.6	
Multiplying fractions	4.6		4.NF.4	5.NF.4 5.NF.6	MP.5, MP.8
	4.7 4.8				
Dividing fractions	4.9 4.10			5.NF.3 5.NF.7	MP.5

Seven of the eight Standards for Mathematical Practice (i.e., 1–3, 5–8) are woven throughout the tasks and are discussed as they relate to the respective tasks. Standard 4, on modeling with mathematics, is interwoven through all the activities, which use visual models as a key tool in reasoning with and understanding fractions.

In addition to fraction notation that features a numerator over a denominator, three particular representations are common in elementary school mathematics to support learning and teaching: *area models, linear models,* and *set models.* As with any mathematical representation, each of these models highlights particular features of the underlying mathematics. Area models, commonly drawn as either rectangles or circles, provide support to consider the equal parts of the whole. Area model drawings as well as physical manipulatives (e.g., fraction pieces, Cuisenaire rods) afford opportunities to compare equal parts, compare the size of the pieces with fractions of different denominators, and consider the meaning of the numerals that represent numerator and denominator. A common area model for fractions in the United States is circles—often used in the context of making real-life connections to pizza. Also common are rectangular area models, often used in the context of fair-sharing with cake or brownies, or as the area of a playground. If a lesson goal is to move across representations, rectangular area models map more easily onto linear models.

Linear models provide some of the same opportunities as area models, and in addition they afford opportunities to consider the role of defining the unit. Number lines of different scales highlight that depending on the length of the unit interval, $1/2$ may appear to be in disparate locations, though it will always be located exactly halfway between the points 0 and 1. Furthermore, number lines are unique in that positive integers, negative integers, and fractions can be located on a single representation as distances from zero rather than with the typical, disjointed treatment they receive in traditional instruction.

Used to represent discrete quantities, set models provide an opportunity to consider fractions as a ratio. For example, a series of 12 circles with 8 circles shaded highlights a fraction as a ratio of the 8 highlighted circles to the 12 total circles. Set models are particularly useful for multiplication of fractions, and in this book we use set models for this purpose. For example, task 4.8 involves a bag of 8 apples in which $1/4$ were rotten. Since a set model may be used to distribute 4 equal groups using 8 total counters, in this case a set model with manipulatives affords particular advantages over area models or number lines.

In this chapter, we present tasks that feature area models, number lines, and set models. We do not take a position that one representation is better than the others; rather, we believe that each highlights particular mathematical properties of fractions and that, therefore, students should have the opportunity to engage with fraction concepts involving all representations.

In addition to the representation, many problems involve a story context. A story context may well support access to the big mathematical ideas when matched with a particular representation. For example, fair-share contexts involving pizzas or cake map onto features of area model representations, while a problem featuring a race, for example, lends itself to considering linear models. At the same time, many rich problems enable access to the big mathematical ideas and engage students in productive mathematical thinking without a supportive story context. We elaborate ways in which the first five tasks could be situated with a lesson plan format that uses the Launch, Explore, Discuss model, following the basic outline for a lesson provided in Van de Walle, Karp, and Bay-Williams (2010). (In their model, "Before," "During," and "After" are used.) In the subsequent cases, the tasks align with topics that the Common Core indicates are to be introduced in the 3–5 grade band but not mastered until the 6–8 grade band. In these cases, we offer only the tasks themselves for the reader's consideration.

Unit Fractions

To develop initial fraction sense, students need to understand *unit fractions* such as $1/5$ or $1/7$. They should make the connection that in any representation involving unit fractions, the denominator signifies the total number of equal parts into which the whole is partitioned, while the numerator signifies one of the total equal parts. In grade 3, standard 3.NF.2 emphasizes that students understand fractions in relation to the number line and be able to represent fractions on one. Unit fractions allow students to engage in foundational concepts—namely, that a whole or unit is divided into equal parts, and the number of equal parts is represented by the denominator. Because the numerator for unit fractions is "1," students can engage in this big mathematical idea that then supports number sense for fractions between 0 and 1, fractions equivalent to 1, and fractions greater than 1.

Fractions pose difficulties for both teaching and learning. By grade 3, students have a repertoire of skills that allows them to count on from any positive whole number—whether that number is 10, 97, or 1,000,000. The numerator and denominator of fraction notation do not follow the same counting rules that young students have relied on for positive whole numbers, making it challenging in teaching and learning to build on students' prior knowledge of the number system. One more than 7 is 8, yet one more than $\frac{1}{7}$ is not $\frac{1}{8}$. Thus prior knowledge of whole numbers can simultaneously enable and constrain students' attempts to understand fractions. Using a variety of visual models such as number lines and manipulatives (e.g., fraction strips, pattern blocks, fraction circles, Cuisenaire rods, graph paper, and double-sided counters) is recommended as a key pedagogical strategy for initial exploration of fraction concepts.

Making fraction strips is an excellent activity to launch initial lessons or discussions about fractions across grades 3–5. In grade 3, making fraction strips can specifically support standard 3.NF.1 that involves students' understanding unit fractions and connecting other fraction representations (e.g., $\frac{3}{4}$) to their part-whole relationship. In task 4.1 (which is modified from NCTM Illuminations, grades 3–5, "Fun with Fractions," Lesson 1), students first make their own fraction strips as a pre-activity to stimulate a discussion around the part-whole relationship of fractions and as a way to make connections to what the numerators and denominators represent (see 3.NF.1). In task 4.2, students are asked to explain which of two fractions is bigger (in the context of a real-world problem) and to use a number line to justify their reasoning. This task addresses several standards in third grade (i.e., 3.NF.1, 2; 3.NF.3d) as well as fourth grade (4.NF.2). With some modifications in wording, task 4.2 can be used to also meet fifth-grade standards, as we explain further in the section that discusses it.

Task 4.1: Making Fraction Strips

At your tables, you have six strips of paper in six different colors. Follow the directions below to make your own fraction kit. You can follow along with the teacher, who will also be making the fraction kit, if you prefer. (Based on the colors of paper available, choose the color for each strip to fill in the blank.)

(*a*) Start with the _____ colored strip of paper. Write the term *one whole* on it.

(*b*) Next, fold the _____ colored strip of paper in two equal pieces. Highlight the fold mark.

(*c*) Fold the _____ colored strip of paper in four equal pieces. Highlight the fold marks.

(*d*) Fold the _____ colored strip of paper in eight equal pieces. Highlight the fold marks.

(*e*) Fold the _____ colored strip of paper in three equal pieces. Highlight the fold marks.

(*f*) Finally, fold the _____ colored strip of paper in six equal pieces. Highlight the fold marks.

Once you are finished, come up with some ideas about which fraction should be used to label the parts of each strip. You might get ideas from books like *Gator Pie* that we have read or from somewhere else. Make sure you have a reason for how you are labeling the parts. Talk to your partner about his or her ideas. Be prepared to share your thinking with the whole group.

Launching the Task—The task can be launched in a variety of ways. For example, teachers could read a book like *Gator Pie* (Mathews 1979), which sets the stage for the concept of sharing a whole in equal pieces in a situation that matters. Instead of launching the task with literature, teachers might use other activities to activate prior knowledge of fractions. For example, students might be asked to free-write in their journals about the question "What do you know about fractions?" This type of open-ended question also serves as an informal pre-assessment. Alternatively, the class as a whole group could brainstorm a list of where one might use fractions in everyday life. Whichever method the teacher chooses to initiate fraction discussion, it is important to facilitate a discussion that highlights the importance of equal pieces as students start working on making their fraction strips.

Task Exploration—Depending on the students, the teacher may choose to co-participate in the fraction strip task. As teacher and students complete each part, the teacher can facilitate a discussion about how to label the parts, emphasizing the need to label pieces with both the word and numeric representation (e.g., one-fourth and $1/4$). Modeling with the fraction strips provides opportunities for the teacher to use the context of mathematics to help students with English language or academic mathematics vocabulary development through the use of such terms as *fold, crease, divide, equal, half, fourths, eighths,* and so on in a naturalistic context.

Alternatively, the teacher can provide students at their tables with both fraction strips and directions for the task, and he or she can let students explore independently first with the option of engaging in informal peer-to-peer interaction about the task. Note that some students might misunderstand directions or start labeling the fraction parts incorrectly. In such cases, it is recommended that teachers wait until the whole-group discussion at the end of the activity and help students self correct instead of pointing out any labeling errors during independent work time. Once all students are done folding and highlighting the pieces, the teacher can facilitate a whole-group discussion that will help students make part-whole connections.

Summarizing Discussion—To summarize students' experiences, ask students the following questions requiring that they use their fraction strips to justify their answers.

- When you folded your fraction strip into two parts, what fraction of the strip did one part represent?
  — Why do you think that?
  — Do others agree or disagree?

- When folding your fraction strip into four parts, what fraction of the strip did one part represent?
  — Tell us why you think that.
  — Do others agree or disagree?

- Show us $3/4$ using your fraction strips.
  — How do you know it's $3/4$?
  — What does the 4 represent?
  — In any fraction with a denominator of 4, will the 4 always mean the same thing?
  — What does the 3 represent?
  — Could this be $3/4$? Why or why not? (Show the class a fraction strip of a different length as a countersuggestion.)

- Now imagine the fraction strips are chocolate bars. One student is given $1/6$ of the chocolate bar and another $1/8$ of the chocolate bar.
  — Who received more chocolate, or did they receive the same amount?
  — Did they each get a fair share? Why or why not?

The fair-share question in the last bulleted item is intended to address another common idea from whole numbers that students bring to studying fractions. Students who have not had the chance to explore fractions with visual models like fraction strips often think that $1/8$ is bigger than $1/6$ because within the domain of whole numbers, 8 is bigger than 6; in fact, the greater the denominator, the more pieces that fit equally into the whole and the smaller any one of those pieces is. Teachers can help students address this by asking them to use fraction strips to justify their answer. Task 4.2 provides an opportunity for students to extend their understanding of unit fractions through the use of a number line.

Task 4.2: Which Fraction Is Bigger?

Two cousins who are at the same grade level but at different schools are having a disagreement about which fraction is bigger—$3/4$ or $3/6$? Celia says that $3/4$ is bigger because that's what her teacher said in school. Sharbel says that $3/6$ is bigger because six is bigger than 4. Whom do you think is right? Write Celia and Sharbel a letter to help them solve their disagreement. They have both learned fractions with number lines at their school, so use number lines to justify your reasoning. You may use your fraction strips to help you think about the number line.

Launching the Task—To engage in task 4.2, students will need some prior knowledge of the connection between number lines and fractions. Teachers can use classroom rulers to help students make connections between the number line and fractions. If this activity is done after task 4.1, teachers can also use the fraction strips created there to make connections to the number line. The fraction strip for the whole can be used as the 0 to 1 block on the number line. Teachers can ask students to come to the board and mark different fractions on the number line, demonstrating how the pieces can be used to generate the intervals on the number line. For example, if a student had to mark $^5/_6$ on the number line, she could use one of the $^1/_6$ pieces to make 6 equal intervals. Teachers may also ask students to predict whether a particular fraction is more or less than $^1/_2$, $^1/_4$, or $^3/_4$ (benchmark fractions) and then use that to estimate and predict where a given fraction might fall on the number line. Such pre-activities will help students get in the mind frame to make connections when they are presented with task 4.2.

Task Exploration—While students are engaging with the problem, the teacher can walk around and help particular students. The teacher might also use this time as an opportunity to conduct informal assessments. This may include making notes about whether students are attending to the numerator and denominator separately or are attending to them together in the context of the whole, as well as noting common patterns in student answers. When representing the fractions on a number line, how are they marking the intervals? If students are working with two different number lines to represent the two different quantities, are both number lines equal in length? Do students understand that implicit to comparing two (or any number of) fractions is the idea that the size of the whole needs to be the same in all cases? These observation notes can help the teacher when she is facilitating the discussion and summarizing the task.

Summarizing Discussion—Once all students have had an opportunity to think about the task and develop an informed opinion about which fraction is larger and why, they are ready to present their thinking. Presentation of student thinking and problem solving can be done individually through activities like a gallery walk with focused note-taking followed by a whole-group discussion. Individual or group presentations to the whole class is another option. After the students or groups selected by the teacher have presented their tasks demonstrating $^3/_4$ as the larger fraction, here are some questions that can be helpful for the summarizing discussion of task 4.2:

- Now that we have proven to ourselves in different ways that $^3/_4$ is larger than $^3/_6$, how should we explain this to Celia and Sharbel?

- If Sharbel still has a hard time understanding why $^3/_6$ is smaller even though 6 is the bigger number, what will you say to him?

- How can you use the number line to help Sharbel with his confusion?

Teachers should be aware that some students may not use the number line to justify their thinking. They may use fraction strips or other strategies. If this happens, teachers might use this strategically in the summarizing discussion to demonstrate different ways in which the problem can be solved, with the emphasis on how students who used the number line solved the problem. Here, the emphasis is not on who is or is not able to solve the problem but rather on the various methods used to solve the problem. How the summarizing discussion is conducted can influence whether students look forward to this phase or shy away from it.

STANDARDS *for Mathematical Practice—Tasks 4.1 and 4.2*

MP.6

The sixth Standard for Mathematical Practice is "Attend to precision" (National Governors Association Center for Best Practices and Council of Chief State School Officers [NGA Center and CCSSO] 2010, p. 7). Some indicators of attending to precision as expressed in this standard are "to communicate precisely to others" and "to use clear definitions in discussion with others and in their own reasoning" (p. 7). In task 4.1, students use multiple, same-sized paper strips and examine how one whole can be broken into many different, yet equal, parts. Students are able to visualize, for example, how $\frac{1}{2}$ of the same whole is the same as $\frac{1}{4} + \frac{1}{4}$. Students' thinking is scaffolded into making the connection and explaining the part-whole relationship of fractions with its corresponding representation. In task 4.2, students have to give justifications for where the fractions are placed on a number line with a 0 to 1 interval identified. Both tasks require that students give clear justifications that support consideration of the underlying mathematical ideas. In task 4.1, *attending to precision* involves discussing the number of equal pieces that fit into a whole (i.e., denominator) and the count of those equal pieces (i.e., numerator). For task 4.2, students may partition a number line from 0 to 1 into both sixths and fourths (or, use two number lines with the same 0-to-1 interval) to identify the six equal lengths (for sixths) and the four equal lengths (for fourths) that fit the same unit, and that while both $\frac{3}{6}$ and $\frac{3}{4}$ involve three equal lengths, the size of those lengths is different. Making student thinking explicit and visible can be challenging in instruction, but it serves a critical function as students form mathematical conjectures and arguments.

MP.7

"Look for and make use of structure" (NGA Center and CCSSO 2010, p. 8). Some indicators of this seventh standard are to "look closely and discern a pattern or structure" and to "see complicated things . . . as single objects or as being composed of several objects" (p. 8). In both tasks 4.1 and 4.2, the contexts of the activity and the discussion are structured so that students are making connections between the concept of fractions and their representations through an examination of patterns in physical models like the fraction strips and number line. Both tasks 4.1 and 4.2 also highlight for students how a single object or whole can be composed of different fractional pieces, an important focus in standard 7.

Fraction Equivalence

In grades 3–5, one key part in developing fraction equivalence is to understand that equivalencies are valid only when fractions are referring to the same whole or unit. In grade 3 (see 3.NF.3) and in grade 4 (see 4.NF.1) there is an emphasis on explaining why fractions are equivalent using such visual models such as manipulatives or number lines. In grade 5, standards 5.NF.1 and 5.NF.2, extend what students learned in previous grades to emphasize the use of equivalent fractions as a strategy to add and subtract fractions.

Task 4.3: Purple Triangle–Gray Rectangle Problem

In figure 4.1, what fraction of the big rectangle is the purple region? Explain how you know. What fraction of the big rectangle is the gray region? Explain how you know.

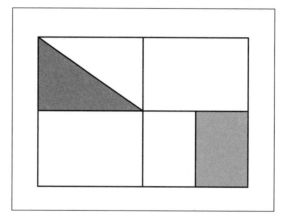

Fig. 4.1. Purple Triangle–Gray Rectangle problem

Teaching fraction equivalency through a task such as the Purple Triangle–Gray Rectangle problem (adapted from Mathematics Teaching and Learning to Teach 2010) is a practical way to address many different ideas simultaneously. From an instructional standpoint, it provides a natural connection between the Number Operations—Fractions and the Geometry domains. In grade 3, there are specific standards in Number and Operations—Fractions (3.NF.3b) and in Geometry (3.G.2) that are addressed through this problem. In grade 4, this task meets the criteria for explaining equivalence using a visual model.

Like other tasks in this book, task 4.3 may be implemented across grades with varied purposes. Grade 3 instruction may engage students in determining the fraction name for either the purple or gray shaded region. For teachers looking for tasks for beginning fractions learners, this particular task problematizes the role of *defining the unit*. At the same time, teachers looking to support students' understanding of equivalent fractions and geometric representations may use the same task to consider the equivalence of the two shaded regions. Because the fraction name depends on defining the unit and because the wording of the problem (e.g., "big rectangle") is intentionally ambiguous, instruction may highlight that the purple-shaded region may be called $1/2$, $1/4$, or $1/8$, depending on what is defined as the whole. Students across grades may productively engage in forming mathematical justifications to support these different responses. Alternatively, students with more experience with fractions may explore fractional equivalence in this problem in order to justify that the purple and gray areas—while *looking* quite different from one another—are equivalent in area.

Launching the Task—As teachers prepare for this task, their focus should be on supporting students in developing an understanding of equivalence, instead of telling students that both the purple triangle and gray rectangle have equivalent areas but different shapes. There are at least two ways to show equivalency: (*a*) both shapes are one-eighth of the whole, or (*b*) both are half of one-fourth. In launching the task, the teacher can facilitate a discussion about how the same whole can be divided into the same number of equal parts in different ways. Everyday items or designs like quilts may be used to draw students' attention to this idea. Students can be supported in developing a flexible understanding of the concept by manipulating one or more shapes—squares, rectangles, circles, triangles, or others.

Task Exploration—Students should work on the problem with a partner or in a small group. One hurdle that students might face with this problem is being able to explain in academic terms what they might intuitively understand or be able to verbalize. For students who might need a different kind of visual support, the teacher might present two separate same-sized rectangles—one with a purple triangle and one with a gray rectangle. It is important to remind students to label the whole as well as the different parts that help them to track the parts in relation to the whole. If they are only looking at the smallest rectangle then that becomes the whole. The purple triangle and gray rectangle are halves in relation to that. However, if the students are looking at the whole rectangle, then the purple triangle and gray rectangle are each one-eighth of the whole. This concept of a *relational whole* is very difficult for students and is key to understanding fraction equivalence.

Summarizing Discussion—Once the students have had a chance to explore and come up with explanations, the teacher should bring the class back together for a whole-group summarizing discussion. Students can be asked to present their thinking in pairs or groups. The teacher can help them to categorize justifications based on one-eighth or one-fourth or other methods that they might use. Some suggested questions for the summarizing discussion are:

- How did you decide which fraction the gray triangle and purple rectangle are?
- Some of you said the regions were one-half. Some of you said the regions were one-eighth. Both explanations could be correct. How can that be?

- When comparing two or more fractions, how can the denominator help us?
- When comparing two or more fractions, how can the numerator help us?

The main focus of the summarizing discussion from the teacher's perspective is to ensure that students' explanations are connected to "the mathematics"—which whole they are focusing on and how that affects naming the part.

STANDARDS *for Mathematical Practice—Task 4.3*

MP.1

"Make sense of problems and persevere in solving them" is the first Standard for Mathematical Practice (NGA Center and CCSSO 2010, p. 6). Task 4.3 provides opportunities for students to have different entry points into the solution, which is one indicator for fulfilling this standard. First, some students might see the solution in relation to halves, while others might see it in eighths and there might be other possibilities as well. Second, the task allows students to use pictures to help conceptualize and solve a problem. Finally, students work to understand the approaches of others to solving complex problems and identify correspondences between different approaches.

MP.3

"Construct viable arguments and critique the reasoning of others" (NGA Center and CCSSO 2010, p. 6). In task 4.3, students are expected to justify their conclusions, communicate them to others, and respond to the arguments of others. The task also allows students to construct arguments using concrete referents such as objects, drawings, diagrams, and actions. Further, while engaging in the summarizing discussion students are expected to listen to the arguments of others, decide whether they make sense, and ask useful questions to clarify or improve the arguments.

MP.6

"Attend to precision" (NGA Center and CCSSO 2010, p. 7). Some indicators of attending to precision are "to communicate precisely to others" and "to use clear definitions in discussions with others and in their own reasoning" (p. 7). In task 4.3, students have to be precise about which whole they are focusing on. Students' understandings are scaffolded into making the connection and explaining the part-whole relationship of fractions with its corresponding representation. The task requires that students give clear definitions about how they know what particular fractions are.

Adding and Subtracting Fractions

One of the key concepts entailed in adding and subtracting fractions is that the joining and separating of parts of a whole is only possible numerically when the parts of the whole are the same size. That is the reason why adding fractions with the same denominator (i.e., like fractions) is relatively easy; the parts being added are the same size. When parts are not the same size, such as adding $^1/_2$ and $^1/_4$ (i.e., unlike fractions), we have to find a *common denominator*. In everyday terms, this means that we are changing the half into two equal fourths to facilitate adding same-sized parts. In other words, finding the common denominator can be analogous to the idea of keeping the units the same during measurement. Just as it is not possible to add centimeters and inches—one must be converted to the other before adding or subtracting them numerically—one must also ensure when working with the same-sized whole having different fractional parts (i.e., fractions with different denominators) that attention is paid to the common denominator or same-sized parts.

In the developmental trajectory of CCSSM, adding and subtracting fractions is a focus in fourth and fifth grades. In fourth grade, the emphasis is on adding and subtracting fractions with like denominators (see 4.NF.3). Task 4.5 is one example of how teaching and learning addition and subtraction of fractions can be accomplished in a connected way within the context of one lesson/problem and does not have to be taught as two separate disconnected lessons. Task 4.6 extends adding and subtracting fractions to unlike denominators (see 5.NF.1; 2) while incorporating common ways that children often think about fractions, frequently referred to as "misconceptions" in research literature.

Task 4.4: Pizza Fractions

Sharbel and Celia ordered take-out pizza of three of the same-sized pizzas—sausage, pepperoni, and cheese. They ate $^3/_8$ of the sausage pizza. They ate $^4/_8$ of the pepperoni pizza, and $^5/_8$ of the cheese pizza. They have pizza left over which they want to store in the boxes. How many of the pizza boxes will they need to keep the leftover pizza? Show your thinking using visual models (pictures or drawings) and write a number sentence to explain your thinking. (Hint: You can write a number sentence to show how much of the pizza was eaten altogether or you can write a number sentence for how much was left over, or any other idea you might have.)

Launching the Task—To prepare students to work on this problem, teachers might choose to have a discussion about what happens at students' homes when they order pizza, what happens with leftover pizza, and other related questions. This provides students who are learning English a larger context to understand the problem when it is presented. It also helps establish a general framework where students understand that people do things differently—such as having different methods of storing pizza.

Task Exploration—After students are presented with the problem and before they start working on it, we recommend taking some time to ensure that students understand what the task is asking them to do. It is helpful to have students identify mathematics vocabulary (e.g., "number sentence") or nonmathematical vocabulary (e.g., "store") that might be confusing. To start working on the problem, one thing that students may do is to draw the three pizzas, represent visually parts that have been eaten and parts that would be left over, and label those representations with their corresponding fractions. Teachers might have students work in groups and use their fraction strips (see task 4.1) to model the quantities. Students should be encouraged to model both aspects of the problem—how much was eaten as well as how much was left over (either through pictures or by using the fraction strips). Since the question asks them to think about how many boxes should be saved, asking students to think about how many whole pizzas were eaten and left over can be a good motivator.

Summarizing Discussion—Once students have had an opportunity to explore the problem, the class should come together for a summarizing discussion. The following are suggested questions for the summarizing discussion:

- Would someone/one of the groups like to explain how you decided how many boxes would be needed to keep the leftover pizza?
- Can somebody share a number sentence that will match this explanation?
- Can anyone explain how much pizza was eaten?
- Can somebody share a number sentence that will match that explanation of how much pizza was eaten?

These summarizing questions are focused on helping students link visual and numerical representations. It will be helpful for students to point out how the denominators of the fractions are the same because all three of these same-sized pizzas were cut into 8 equal-sized slices. The wording can be modified to extend this problem to introduce adding and subtracting unlike denominators: "Now imagine that the pizza store made a mistake and cut the pizzas into different numbers of slices. Two of the pizzas were cut into 8 equal-sized slices and one was cut into 16 equal-sized slices."

- How could we figure out how much pizza was eaten then? How would the fraction change?
- Would the number of boxes to keep the leftover pizza change? Can you explain your thinking?

This task is very productive in helping students begin to make connections between the idea of a common denominator and equivalence; when we modify the size of the parts in dealing with a whole, the size of the part changes but the whole does not change. This is an important concept as students begin to wrestle with problems involving unlike denominators, and it can be a good warm-up for a more complex problem involving unlike denominators such as task 4.5. The design of task 4.5 is motivated by how children think about unlike fractions in the initial phases of being presented with that concept. Often children will overlook the "size" of the parts and focus on "number." In task 4.5, Celia being upset over Sharbel's three helpings versus her two helpings is intended to address thinking that is focused on *quantity* instead of *parts*.

Task 4.5: Who Drank More Lemonade?

After a pizza party, Celia and Sharbel both decided they were thirsty and wanted some lemonade. Sharbel took out measuring cups to make sure they got exactly the same amount. They only had two measuring cups—$1/2$ cup and $1/4$ cup. Celia took two helpings—one helping of $1/2$ cup of juice and then $1/4$ cup more. Sharbel took three helpings of the $1/4$ cup. Celia was upset because she thought Sharbel was not being fair and took more lemonade. Do you think Sharbel was being fair or unfair? Show your thinking using a number line and one other representation. (Hint: You might find your fraction strips helpful for this task.)

Launching the Task—To introduce the task, the teacher might choose to bring in measuring cups and have a pre-discussion about measuring cups. Students might explore how the sizes of the cups relate to each other to develop prior knowledge if students have not had experience with measuring cups.

Exploring the Task—Students might continue to use the physical cups to explain their thinking. While the measuring cups will help students see the practical resolution to the problem, fraction strips or other tools can be used to connect visual and numerical representations.

Summarizing Discussion—Suggested questions for a summarizing discussion are:

- After exploring the problem, do you think Sharbel was being fair or unfair?
- How can you explain that to Celia so that she is convinced? Can you write an equation that will convince Celia that they are both indeed drinking the same amount of lemonade? For example:

$$1/2 + 1/4 = 1/4 + 1/4 + 1/4$$
$$1/4 + 1/4 + 1/4 = 1/4 + 1/4 + 1/4$$

STANDARDS *for Mathematical Practice—Tasks 4.4 and 4.5*

MP.7

The seventh Standard for Mathematical Practice is "Look for and make use of structure" (NGA Center and CCSSO 2010, p. 8); it hinges on students attending to and figuring out a pattern or structure. In both tasks 4.5 and 4.6, students are attending to how to put together one whole with same and different-size parts. In task 4.6, they are also wrestling with how to approach the problem and how to structure it when talking about the same whole yet different-size parts.

Developing Understanding of Multiplying Fractions

In grades 3–5, the focus of teaching multiplication of fractions is to introduce the concept through exploring multiplication of fractions by whole numbers (e.g., $1/4 \times 20$) and fractions by fractions (e.g., $1/2 \times 1/4$). Fluency with fraction multiplication is not expected until sixth grade within the CCSSM framework. The main concept that students should understand in the 3–5 grade band is that the context of the problem drives whether we are looking at an equal group of fractional parts, or the fractional part of a set. For example, consider task 4.6.

Task 4.6: Clock Problem

Luz reads for $1/4$ hour every night. After 8 nights, how much total time has she been reading?

Depending on how students approach the task, this problem can be done as repeated addition. The affordance of task 4.6 is to support students' development of multiplying fractions in the context of an area model represented as a circle. Tasks 4.7 and 4.8 use the same numbers and help students to understand the importance of context in trying to set up a problem.

Task 4.7: Leftover Juice

At the end of your birthday party, there were 8 glasses of juice left over. There was $1/4$ cup of juice in each of those glasses. How many cups of juice were left over?

The context of this problem is also geared towards being represented as eight $1/4$s coming together using a repeated addition or counting up strategy. While the result will always be 2, an understanding of how different representations are possible will be key in helping students be successful with multiplying fractions in middle school. In the course of exploring other similar problems, students may notice the relationship between multiplying the numerator with the whole number (e.g., $\frac{1}{4} \times 8 = \frac{1 \times 8}{4}$). Students may call upon particular representations to support equivalent answers of $^8/_4$, or 8 counts of $^1/_4$, or 2.

Task 4.8: Edible Apples

Out of a bag of 8 apples, $^1/_4$ were rotten. How many apples would still be good to eat? Use pictures, counters, or numbers to explain your thinking.

The context in the rotten apples problem is geared towards thinking in terms of fractional parts of a set. Given a set of 8 apples, one would have to put those in four equal groups of two each and then see how many would be in three of those groups to solve for the edible apples.

To extend discussions of multiplying fractions by fractions (e.g., $^1/_4 \times ^1/_8$), models such as fraction strips can be used to demonstrate how fractional parts are further subdivided. Story problems allow students the opportunity to drive their understanding grounded in a meaningful context. From an instructional perspective, story problems involving unit fractions—such as those in task 4.8—may provide an entry point into discussion of multiplication and division of fractions.

STANDARDS *for Mathematical Practice—Tasks 4.6 through 4.8*

MP.5

"Use appropriate tools strategically" is the fifth Standard for Mathematical Practice (NGA Center and CCSSO 2010, p. 7). The main focus of this practice standard is to help students consider the available tools when solving a mathematics problem. This becomes particularly important when teaching fraction multiplication, as not every type of representational tool is suitable for every fraction multiplication problem. For example, in task 4.7, the Leftover Juice problem, the amount of juice is a continuous quantity, so using a circle area model to represent the problem may be more appropriate than counters. Since we want to support children in selecting the tool that is most useful and understandable to them, teachers should allow a variety of representations. The importance of helping students to understand how different representational tools can have a different impact on their thinking about the problem cannot be emphasized enough.

MP.8

"Look for and express regularity in repeated reasoning" (NGA Center and CCSSO 2010, p. 8). The focus of this practice standard is to give students the opportunity to explore mathematical tasks with common repeating elements and to help students make observations about generalities that might apply. For example, after several experiences with representing a solution path with pictures and numeric expressions (e.g., $1/4 + 1/4 + 1/4 + 1/4 + 1/4 + 1/4 + 1/4 + 1/4$, for the clock and the juice problems) students can be asked to look for a pattern that might lead them to see that $1/4 + 1/4 + 1/4 + 1/4 + 1/4 + 1/4 + 1/4 + 1/4 = 8/4$.

Developing Understanding of Dividing Fractions

In grades 3–5, the focus of teaching division of fractions is to introduce the concept through exploring division of whole numbers by fractions (e.g., $20 \div 1/5$) and fractions by whole numbers (e.g., $1/2 \div 3$). Similar to fraction multiplication, fluency with dividing fractions is not expected until sixth grade within the CCSSM framework. To get students oriented, it is helpful to have a discussion reviewing strategies that students might use for whole number *partitive and measurement* division. Consider tasks 4.9 and 4.10.

Task 4.9: Brownie Problem

You want to share 4 brownies equally with 9 friends. If you want to give each friend $1/2$ a brownie, will 4 brownies be enough? Explain your thinking in two ways.

Task 4.9 is an example of a partitive fraction division problem. Some students may choose to use division strategies of repeated subtraction. What is most important is that students are able to explain how they are thinking. Similar to the previous section on multiplying fractions, it will be important to help students understand which representation (e.g., area model in this case), will be best to explain their thinking. Servings of food such as brownies can be a good place to start exploring fractions and division. As suggested throughout, students should be encouraged to draw and model the problems.

Task 4.10: Making Puppets

You want to put on a puppet show with your friends. You have 2 meters of fabric. Each puppet needs $1/4$ m of fabric. How many puppets can you make with the fabric you have? Show your thinking in at least two ways. One of them should be a number line.

Task 4.10 is an example of a measurement fraction division problem. In this case, a linear or bar model will be supportive of students' problem solving. Again, what is most important is that students are encouraged to explain how they are thinking about the problem. Once again, connecting this problem to previous work with fraction strips may prove fruitful.

STANDARDS *for Mathematical Practice—Tasks 4.9 and 4.10*

MP.5

"Use appropriate tools strategically" (NGA Center and CCSSO 2010, p. 7). This practice requires students to consider the available tools when solving a problem. As discussed in the section on multiplying fractions, division of fractions is also heavily dependent on the context. Helping students develop an understanding of how different models of representations can either support their thinking about a problem or confuse them is one way these tasks can be incorporated into a summarizing discussion.

Chapter 5
Measurement and Data

The word *measurement* has its roots in the Greek word *metron*, which is also the origin of the standard measure unit, *meter*. Despite the variation across individuals, body parts (such as the length of an arm or a foot or of a stride) were used in ancient civilizations as measurement units. Formal measurement practices eventually became characterized by the standard units of measure we use today, such as the feet and yards customary in U.S. culture or the meters used elsewhere in the world. The word *data* is the plural form of the Latin word *datum*, and it refers to a set of facts or information. Both measurement and data provide elementary students with opportunities to observe their world and the objects in it through a mathematical lens.

This chapter takes a problem-solving approach to measurement and data, and it makes use of manipulatives and written representations to accomplish this. As in other chapters, we will take a cross-grade perspective when appropriate to consider problems that address particular Common Core State Standards for Mathematics (CCSSM). In one of the areas we identify below, geometric measurement, standards are written with distinct attention to each grade level. For this reason, we provide three tasks in this section, each of which corresponds to standards in grade 3, 4, or 5. Nonetheless, these tasks may also be implemented across grades to address particular needs of students.

This book's appendix provides a progression of the standards across grade levels. The Measurement and Data domain begins in kindergarten–grade 2, when students explore measurable attributes of objects, classify objects, and explore time (see Schwartz 2013). Moreover, standards beginning in kindergarten focus on representing and interpreting *categorical* data that are sorted into different discrete categories (such as birth month, species of pets, or ice cream flavors) and are often represented using picture graphs or bar graphs. Standards beginning in grade 2 focus on representing and interpreting *measurement* data in standard units of measure. Measurement data refer to the use of tools or representations featuring consistent numeric units and intervals assigned to attributes of the world around us. This allows other people—whether in the same room or across the world—to understand and communicate the exact properties of the object being measured based on an established scale (e.g., using a meter stick—which is actually just a number line with particular standardized units—to measure the dimensions of a room). Standards in grades 3–5 continue to emphasize both categorical and measurement data. Grade 3 standards continue with representing and interpreting categorical data, although grade 3 is the final grade in which CCSSM refers to categorical data. Representing and interpreting measurement data continue through grade 5. The work involved with the Measurement and Data domain directly supports work in grades 6–12 involved with both the Geometry and the Statistics and Probability domains.

In organizing the standards across grade levels, we identify three distinct areas that need attention when addressing the Measurement and Data domain in grades 3–5:

(1) Measurement and conversion

(2) Geometric measurement

(3) Representing and interpreting data

What follows are tasks that can support the development of thinking in each of these three areas: measurement and conversion (tasks 5.1 and 5.2), geometric measurement (tasks 5.3, 5.4, and 5.5), and representing and interpreting data (tasks 5.6 and 5.7).

Table 5.1 provides a reference for content area, tasks, content standards, and mathematical practices. While we target particular content and practice standards here, the tasks may be extended to address other standards within the Measurement and Data or other domains.

Table 5.1

Content areas, grade-level standards, and mathematical practice standards met by the tasks in chapter 4

Content Areas	Tasks	Grade 3 Standards	Grade 4 Standards	Grade 5 Standards	Standards for Mathematical Practice
Measurement and conversion	5.1	3.MD.2	4.MD.1 4.MD.2	5.MD.1	MP.2, MP.3
	5.2	3.MD.1	4.MD.2		
Geometric measurement	5.3	3.MD.5 3.MD.6 3.MD.7 3.MD.8	4.MD.3		MP.5, MP.7
	5.4		4.MD.5 4.MD.6 4.MD.7		
	5.5			5.MD.3 5.MD.4 5.MD.5	
Represent and interpret data	5.6	3.MD.3			MP.4, MP.6, MP.7
	5.7	3.MD.4	4.MD.4	5.MD.2	

A foundational component of measurement data is the idea of an interval (e.g., the length of an interval from 0 inches to 54 inches) as opposed to a discrete quantity (e.g., 54 candies). Components of measurement tools also may inadvertently be treated as discrete positions. This is illustrated in figure 5.1 with the treatment of a number line as continuous intervals (fig. 5.1a) as opposed to a series of discrete points (fig. 5.1b). The interval from 2 inches to 7 inches on a ruler is 5 inches because it represents five unit intervals. Many students come to understand a number line instead as a series of discrete—and possibly disconnected—points. This is exemplified by students conceptualizing five by using a count of tick marks instead of a length of five unit intervals (fig. 5.1b). Such a distinction is in no way trivial, as students' understanding of continuous quantities supports their future work with representations in algebra and calculus. Figure 5.1a reflects a conceptual understanding of interval and measurement that is consistent with, for example, further partitioning each unit interval in half to locate the position of mixed numbers (e.g., $2^1/_2$, $3^1/_2$); a discrete count of tick marks is not consistent with locating these same mixed numbers. For an activity that engages students in considering the role of tick marks on a number line, see sample tasks A and B in chapter 1.

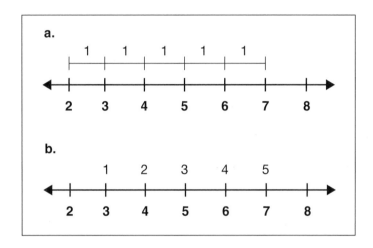

Fig. 5.1. Number lines interpreted as a series of unit intervals (a)
and as a series of discrete points (b)

Measurement and Conversion

A core idea in measurement is the use of units. The Measurement and Data standards for grades 3–5 highlight the importance of particular standard units, including feet and inches, metric units, and units of time. Specifically, students in these grades explore units within a single system (e.g., feet and inches). One foot, for example, is equivalent to 12 inches, whereas one meter is equivalent to 100 centimeters, and one hour is equivalent to 60 minutes. Units within a given system involve different exchanges. The standards in grades 3–5 focus on both familiarity with these systems and conversions within them.

By grade 3, students have familiarity with measuring their height, and many will know their own heights in feet and inches. Nonetheless, students may have little experience in considering heights expressed in different units within the same system. The first task presented here engages students in considering units within the system of feet and inches.

Another system of units involves measuring time. Understanding time and units of time is a critical skill for all children, even if digital clocks are ubiquitous in mainstream U.S. culture. Understanding time involves seamless conversion across three units: hours, minutes, and seconds. Unlike the units involved in the metric system, in which powers of 10 differentiate units, units of time do not lend themselves in obvious ways to landmark numbers or conversions. In fact, the clock face itself does not feature the number 0, and 12 is often considered to be a "starting place" for the hour and minute hands of the clock. Understanding time poses considerable challenges for many children, and at the same time engaging students in understanding time is a rich source of problem solving that supports the development of mathematical ideas in measurement, fractions, and geometry.

Partitioning a clock face into equal units supports children's understanding of time and of the vocabulary associated with time, and it also draws upon their developing understanding of fractions. For example, partitioning a clock face in half creates two equal sections, each of which represents half an hour. Partitioning the clock face once more can create four equal sections, each of which represents a quarter of an hour (see fig. 5.2). In grades 1 and 2, standards focus on telling time and, in particular, on how the second of any two consecutive numerals on the clock (1–12) marks the endpoint of a five-minute interval. The vocabulary of "half" and "quarter" refer to a specific unit of time, 60 minutes, something that is not immediately visible on the clock face. An activity (e.g., task 5.2) in which the clock face is partitioned supports children in associating these fraction words with a whole and parts of a whole. In particular, this task makes explicit that in our culture, we use the word "quarter" to refer both to 25 cents ($^1/_4$ of 100 cents) and 15 minutes ($^1/_4$ of 60 minutes). We commonly refer to a "quarter" without referencing the whole, because when already working within an established system of units, the whole is "known" and we do not need to. The common cultural lack of reference to the whole when using the word "quarter" renders this word ambiguous to young learners.

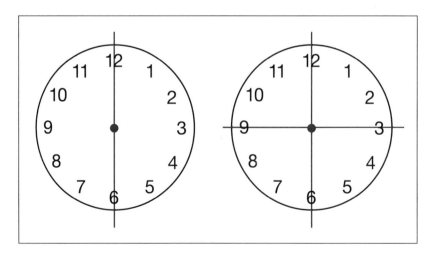

Fig. 5.2. Partitioned clock faces

Task 5.1: Measuring Height

Esha, Rose, and Ben are classmates. For homework, their teacher asked each student to measure his or her height. They are having a debate about who is tallest and who is shortest. Esha measured her height to be 5 feet. Rose measured her height to be 54 inches. Ben measured his height to be $4^1/_2$ feet. Who is tallest? Who is shortest? How do you know? Write a letter to them to help them understand your thinking.

Launching the Task—Engage students in a discussion about measuring heights. Many will know their own height and may be able to report this to the class. To launch the task, depending on the amount of time allocated, you may measure the heights of a few students to engage the class in considering the system of feet and inches. Alternatively, student pairs can measure each other's heights. Remind them about tools they might use such as a ruler, tape, or yardstick. (Kits with different measuring tools can be prepared in advance for students.) You may also use the names and heights of a few students in your classroom in place of those provided in the problem above.

Ask students what they notice about feet and inches. Students may notice that many of the students in the class are around the same height. If students do not bring it up, ask them how many inches are in a foot, and then how many inches are in two feet. Engage students in considering whether they express height in feet, inches, or both feet and inches. Present the task to students. Explain to students that, like they just did, Esha, Rose, and Ben all measured their heights, but in looking at the numbers they recorded, are confused as to who is the tallest.

Task Exploration—As students work in pairs to write a letter to help Esha, Rose, and Ben understand their relative heights, encourage them to draw a picture, create a table of values, or measure the actual lengths with a tape measure to support their arguments. For students who need additional support, ask them what they notice about the three heights: 5 feet, 54 inches, and $4^1/_2$ feet? Are they all in the same units? Students may be able to quickly determine that Esha (5 feet) is taller than Ben ($4^1/_2$ feet), though determining Rose's height (54 inches) relative to Esha's and Ben's will be more difficult. As students work, note how they choose to represent the relative heights for the summarizing discussion.

Summarizing Discussion—Begin the discussion by asking students whether there was a comparison that was easier to make. Students may indicate that Esha was clearly taller than Ben. Provide supporting questions to highlight the role of *units* in making this comparison.

- • Why was this comparison easier to make?
- • What units did Esha use to record her height? What about Ben?
- • What units did Rose use to record her height?

You may wish to have some groups present to the class their letters in which they provide an explanation for how they know Rose is the same height as Ben. Alternatively, you may wish to post letters along the wall and have a gallery walk in which students are able to read the different letters. To conclude the discussion, engage students in considering that we can express our heights in either feet or inches. A number line representation of both feet and inches will provide additional support for equivalence of Ben's and Rose's heights. In the discussion, focus on the equivalence of 12 inches to one foot.

Task 5.2: Quarter of an Hour

Joseph's father told him that the time was a quarter past 7. Joseph wrote down the time as 7:25 because he knows that a quarter means 25. What do you think Joseph was thinking? How would you help Joseph?

Launching the Task—Ask students what they know about time. Children will likely have familiarity with the times associated with their own routines, such as getting up in the morning, lunchtime, or bedtime. Draw attention to the analog clock in your classroom, or use a clock manipulative. What does each of the numbers on the clock mean? Using the clock manipulative, position the hour and minute hands and ask students to identify different times (e.g., 3:00, 4:30, 2:45, 8:55). If students do not bring it up, ask them how many minutes are in an hour. What about half an hour? Present the task to students.

Task Exploration—Unlike many common activities involving time, this particular task involves mathematical argument as a core component. Instead of simply asking students to identify the time that corresponds to a quarter past 7, the task requires argumentation involving both measurement and fractions. As you circulate among the different groups, ascertain whether students are able to identify the time corresponding to "a quarter past 7" as 7:15. Using either a drawing of a clock or the clock manipulatives, engage students in considering how many quarters of an hour are in a full hour. To support struggling students, provide them with a worksheet featuring a clock, such as the one in figure 5.3a, and encourage them to record on it the values for the number of minutes. Consider also representing time on a number line (a timeline), which may further support the idea of the "five-ness" of the intervals between consecutive numerals on the clock (fig. 5.3b). This will also provide an entry into discussing the lack of zero on the clock face.

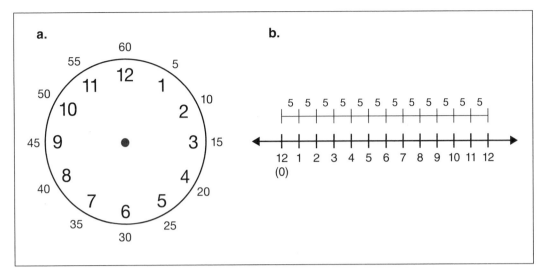

Fig. 5.3. Representations of time

Summarizing Discussion—The discussion for task 5.2 should focus on the relationship of time measurement to fraction words associated with the clock.

Ask students the following questions:

- Where is a half on the clock? Can someone partition the clock in half? (A clock face may be partitioned in half in infinitely many ways, but here we refer to half on the clock as the bisection from 12 to 6.)

- Where is a quarter on the clock? Can someone draw another line to show quarters?

- How many quarters are in an hour? How many quarters are in a dollar?

- Why is 25 cents a quarter of a dollar, but 15 minutes is a quarter of an hour? Why are these quarters different?

Draw students' attention to what is the same about a quarter in each case, namely, that a quarter corresponds to $^1/_4$ and means that there are 4 equal parts that fit into a whole. Continue to ask questions to emphasize the relationship of parts to the whole, and that in each case (time and money) the whole is different.

- What is the **whole** when we talk about a quarter of an hour? [The whole is an hour, or 60 minutes.]

- What is the **whole** when we talk about a quarter of a dollar? [The whole is a dollar, or 100 cents.]

- Why are these two meanings of quarters—time and money—different numbers?

- Are there other ways we use the word "quarter" that represent a different quantity?

As an extension, ask students whether they have seen packages of a pound of butter that come in four equal sticks. Ask them whether they know how many ounces is equivalent to a pound of butter; if they do not know, tell them that 1 pound of butter is 16 ounces. How much is a quarter pound of butter? To conclude, encourage students to articulate how the whole relates to the quarter in each case: $1/4$ of an hour is 15 minutes, $1/4$ of a dollar is 25 cents, and $1/4$ of a pound of butter is 4 ounces.

STANDARDS *for Mathematical Practice—Tasks 5.1 and 5.2*

MP.2

"Reason abstractly and quantitatively" is the second Standard for Mathematical Practice (National Governors Association Center for Best Practices and Council of Chief State School Officers [NGA Center and CCSSO] 2010, p. 6). Task 5.1 engages students in comparing quantities using different units (feet and inches) within the same system. The Common Core State Standards underscore the importance of considering both the units involved while at the same time reasoning quantitatively. In comparing heights measured in either feet or inches, students consider both quantitative comparisons of greater than and less than. At the same time, the role of conversion in the problem engages students in considering mathematical properties of the heights provided in the task through coordination across the two different types of units.

MP.3

"Construct viable arguments and critique the reasoning of others" (NGA Center and CCSSO 2010, p. 6). A task such as task 5.2 requires students to formulate mathematical arguments to consider the reasoning of others (in this case, to consider the reasoning of Joseph, the character from the task). In doing so, students formulate justifications both for Joseph's response and for alternative responses generated by classmates.

Geometric Measurement

Geometric measurement brings together two domains of mathematics that students have been exploring since kindergarten (and informally from well before this): geometry and number. In geometric measurement, we use consistent measuring techniques to assign numbers to particular attributes of geometric figures. For each grade level in grades 3–5, the Common Core State Standards focus on a different measurable attribute. Typically this involves the use of a tool, such as a ruler, tape measure, or protractor. Many students can become confused when measuring perimeter, surface area, and volume by the fact that linear measure is used in calculations even when the measure itself (e.g., volume) is not linear; this issue is explored in the tasks below. Unlike other areas within the measurement standards, the CCSSM standards for geometric measurement are different for each grade in grades 3–5.

Standards for geometric measurement in grade 3 focus on two attributes of two-dimensional shapes: area and perimeter. In task 5.3, students design a garden using grid paper or square manipulatives such as colored tiles. The number of squares or tiles (in this case, 24) to be used is dictated by the task. Because the number of squares is set, the area for any garden design remains the same. The need to enclose the garden with a fence draws attention to another attribute of two-dimensional figures—perimeter. Despite the fact that the area remains the same for each garden design, the amount of fence needed changes depending on the configuration of the garden. This type of task emphasizes that area and perimeter are unique attributes, each of which is measurable.

Standards for geometric measurement in grade 4 focus in particular on understanding concepts of angle and measurement of angles. While one interpretation of these standards may be, for example, to distribute protractors to students and direct them to measure angles with precision, we provide task 5.4 as another way to explore the use of the protractor, a tool that students frequently have difficulty using initially. Students in grade 4 are familiar with the idea of measuring various attributes of objects, such as length or weight. While many may not yet be familiar with measuring angles, they have experience exploring angles of different sizes with manipulatives such as pattern blocks. Task 5.4 is launched by engaging in a discussion on different attributes to measure on a series of rays, including rays that share an endpoint to form an angle. Even without using the mathematical vocabulary of *right*, *acute*, or *obtuse* angles, students may notice that some angles are smaller, some are larger, and others resemble the corners of a room. After a description of the different lines and angles and a discussion of different tools for measuring, students are introduced to the protractor and explore its properties. Such a task lays the groundwork for content that continues through high school, when students encounter similarity, right triangles, and trigonometry in the Geometry domain.

Standards for geometric measurement in grade 5 focus on volume, one attribute of three-dimensional solid figures. In task 5.5, students explore the volume of various rectangular prisms made from poster board. Block manipulatives serve as cubic units to measure the volume of each box. The task allows students to explore volume, and use two rectangular prisms of equivalent volume but different dimensions to further develop their understanding of volume. In particular, students may use this task to explore three-dimensional properties of volume despite the fact that three linear measures—length, width, and height—may be used to determine the volume.

Task 5.3: Ethan's Garden (Area and Perimeter)

Ethan is creating a fenced-in section for his new garden. He wants the garden to be 24 square feet to fit all of the plants he wants to grow. How many different ways can he make the garden? How much fence does he need for each different design? What is the largest amount of fence he would need? What is the smallest? He has only one gate, so all parts of the garden must be connected.

Launching the Task—Engage students in considering the relative sizes of community gardens or other gardens they have seen, and why many gardens have fences around them. Students in suburban or rural areas may be familiar with gardens tended by family or friends. Students in urban areas may have seen community gardens in their neighborhoods. Depending on where they live, people may have different reasons for needing fencing in their gardens. In rural areas, fences may be needed to keep out rabbits or other animals, whereas more urban areas may have fences so that dogs or playing children cannot disturb the plantings. Children may also have ideas of different plants that may grow in particular areas.

You may also engage students in a discussion about area. Consider using square tiles or multi-link cubes to make rectangular arrays; discuss how an array that has 6 tiles in each row and 4 tiles in each column has an area of 24 tiles. Have students arrange the tiles in different configurations such that their sides are touching. Use a piece of string and have students predict which configuration will need the most string to go "around" the shape and which one needs the least. Present the task to students.

Task Exploration—The goal for students is to design gardens with an area of 24 square feet and to determine the different amounts of fencing needed for different configurations. Students may choose to represent each square foot using grid paper, colored tiles, or another manipulative that will allow them to count the number of feet for the perimeter. They may quickly discover that the garden need not be arranged as a rectangle, and they may have fun designing different and oddly shaped gardens. The only requirement is that Ethan can access the garden with the one gate he has (or, in other words, that all square units be connected on at least one side). Figure 5.4 provides some examples students may generate. (Note that we provide these examples to alert teachers of possible configurations and not to suggest they be presented to students.)

Summarizing Discussion—Begin the discussion by asking students how many different ways they found to configure Ethan's garden. You may have students walk around the room to observe their classmates' garden representations, or you may use a document projector for representations on grid paper. Raise questions such as the following:

- Who thinks they have created a design that uses the least amount of fence?
- Who thinks they have created a design that uses the most amount of fence?
- What is the same about the different garden designs?
- What is different about some of the garden designs?

If students do not bring it up, draw their attention to the fact that each and every garden design is 24 square feet. Or, in other words, the area for every garden design is the same. The amount of fence Ethan needs depends on the design of the garden. Introduce students to the word *perimeter* as the word mathematicians use to describe the distance around the edge of something. In this case, the perimeter refers to the amount of fencing (in feet) Ethan needs.

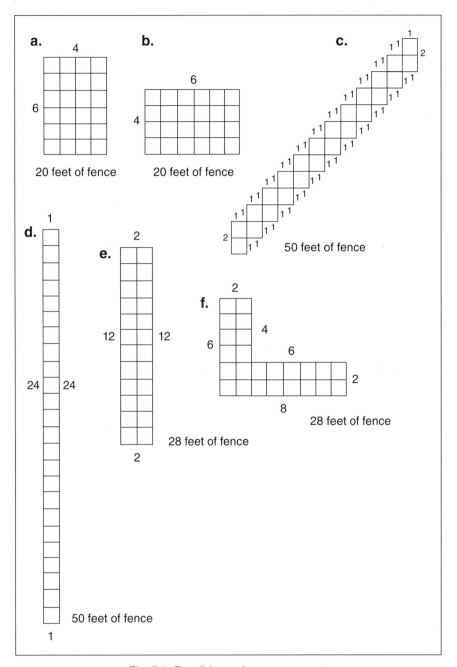

Fig. 5.4. Possible garden arrangements

Ask students to share other observations about their gardens. To connect to a standard in the Operations and Algebraic Thinking domain, draw attention to gardens such as gardens (*a*) and (*b*) in figure 5.4. Each garden is a rectangle that has two edges that are 6 feet long and two edges that are 4 feet long, yet the gardens are oriented differently. In this case, the area and perimeter are the same for the two garden designs, even though the designs are different.

Task 5.4: Rulers and Protractors

What are the different ways we can measure the items in figure 5.5?

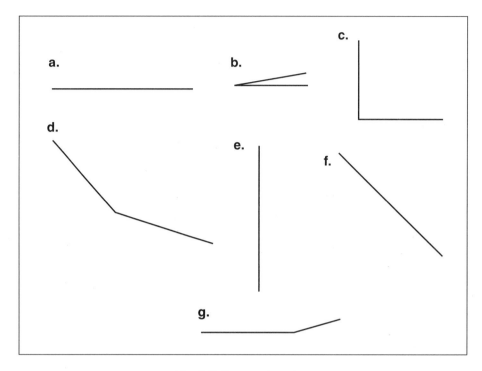

Fig. 5.5. Rays and angles

Launching the Task—Engage students in considering different tools they are familiar with that are used for measuring. Students most likely have experience in being weighed on a scale, using a ruler or tape measure to measure height, and using a thermometer to measure temperature. While students may not be familiar with the use of the word *degree* as it applies to angle measure, they are likely familiar with the word in other contexts. To support mathematical vocabulary, ask students to give examples of what they know about the word *degree*. Students may refer to a high school or college degree, degrees used to measure temperature, or a degree of difficulty. Indicate that when measuring angles, mathematicians use units called "degrees," and that this may be a new and different meaning of the word.

Present students with the lines and angles featured in figure 5.5. Ask them to volunteer different ways they could measure properties of these shapes. Students will likely volunteer using a ruler to measure the length of lines provided. Ask them whether there are other properties that they can see and describe. If necessary, draw their attention to the shapes (*a*) and (*b*). How are they different? How do they resemble different things in the world?

Task Exploration—Ask students whether they know about a tool for measuring angles. Introduce them to the protractor (see fig. 5.6). Let them know that like a ruler, a protractor is used for measuring. Yet while a ruler is used for linear measure (in inches, centimeters, etc.), a protractor is used to measure angles. In pairs or small groups, students can explore the protractor and even attempt to measure the angles in figure 5.5. Allow students to use both the ruler and the protractor to measure different attributes of the rays and angles.

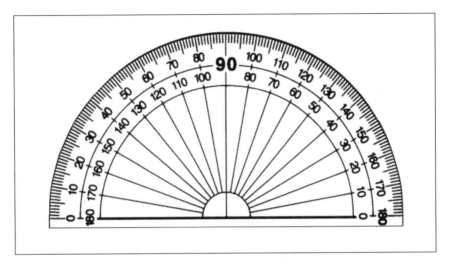

Fig. 5.6. Example of a protractor

Summarizing Discussion—Prompt students to share their observations about the protractor through questions such as the following:

- What do you notice about the protractor?
- What numbers are featured? What do you notice about those numbers?
- What could you measure with the ruler? What could you measure with the protractor?

Students may notice that, like a ruler, the protractor features different lines to help measure. They may also notice that values on the protractor increase and decrease by 10s, and that all numbers except for 90 (depending on the protractor) are featured twice. The numbers on the protractor refer to the unit we use to measure angles: degrees. Students will also likely observe that the number 90 corresponds to the angle that resembles a corner. Indicate to students that these are special angles called *right angles*, and that each right angle is 90 degrees.

The following task is adapted from one in a volume from Van de Walle, Karp, and Bay-Williams (2010, p. 382).

Task 5.5: Box Comparisons

What is the volume of the various boxes that your group has?

Task Preparation—This task requires prior preparation of materials. Using poster board or card stock, prepare a variety of small boxes. To measure the dimensions of the boxes, use the same blocks that students will use as they engage in the task. (Commercially available 1-inch colored cubes or centicubes work well.) Suggested box dimensions (L × W × H) include the following:

$$2 \times 2 \times 4 \qquad 5 \times 4 \times 4$$
$$2 \times 4 \times 2 \qquad 3 \times 9 \times 9$$
$$6 \times 3 \times 4 \qquad 5 \times 5 \times 3$$

Teachers should not feel limited to using these dimensions, and they also may wish to make some boxes that have the same volume but different length-to-width-to-height configurations. Figure 5.7 displays how to use the poster board to draw the dimensions. After cutting out the box on the exterior solid lines, cut the interior solid lines, fold the box on the dotted lines, and then wrap the corner squares to the outside and tape them to the sides.

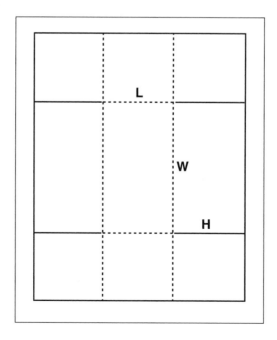

Fig. 5.7. Using poster board to make boxes of different volumes
(from Van de Walle, Karp, and Bay-Williams 2010, p. 382)

Launching the Task—Present the students with a box or container and ask them to describe different properties they could measure. Students will likely indicate the volume of the box (among other properties, such as length, width, and height), though they may not use the word *volume*. Ask students when it is useful to know the size of a container or a box. Students may indicate such situations as a box for storing toys or a container for milk or juice. Introduce the word *volume* to them (if they do not already know it in this context) as the word used to describe how much may fit inside a container.

Present students with two different boxes and ask them to describe the boxes. For example, you may choose one that is markedly taller or longer than the other. Students may begin to describe the different dimensions of the boxes using informal language, such as *deeper* or *taller*. To further support students, introduce to them the words *length*, *width*, and *height* as they share their observations, and write these terms on the board.

Present the task to students: Which box has the greatest volume? You may wish to solicit predictions from students about which box has the greatest volume and which the least. Alternatively, as students begin to work in small groups or in pairs, use these questions to assess them informally as they work. Indicate to students that they can use blocks to measure the dimensions of the boxes.

Task Exploration—Allow students to work in small groups on the box comparisons. As you check in with different groups, ask students questions such as the following:

- Which box has the greatest volume?
- Which has the least volume?
- Do any of the boxes have the same volume?

Summarizing Discussion—Begin the discussion by asking students how they found the volume of the boxes. Some students may have placed blocks in the box and then counted each block in order to determine how many blocks fit inside. Alternatively, other students may have found the dimensions of the box in terms of length, width, and height. Ask questions such as the following:

- How did you determine the volume of each box?
- Which box was the biggest?
- Which box was the smallest?

Select particular boxes (or all of them if time permits) and record these on the board by having students come up and write the volume of the boxes. Alternatively, teachers can have students volunteer the dimensions for the different boxes if they measured those dimensions (see table 5.2 for an example of how to record these in a table). If using a subset of boxes, include two boxes that have the same volume but are differently configured, as well as the boxes with the biggest and smallest dimensions.

Table 5.2
*Example of a table to organize students'
measurements of volume*

Box	Volume	Length	Width	Height
A				
B				
...				

Draw attention to the two boxes with the same volume that are differently configured. Ask students:

- If these boxes look so different from each other, how can they possibly have the same volume?

In the ensuing discussion, remind students that volume is determined computationally by three dimensions: length, width, and height. If the students do not state it explicitly, state that volume can be found by multiplying length by width by height, using the values in the table as examples of this. Using the dimensions written on the board, guide the discussion so that students talk about how, for example, one container is as tall as the other container is wide.

STANDARDS *for Mathematical Practice—Tasks 5.3 through 5.5*

MP.5

"Use appropriate tools strategically" (NGA Center and CCSSO 2010, p. 7). The strategic use of tools is a fundamental part of measurement. Tasks 5.4 and 5.5 each engage students in the exploration and use of particular tools in order to measure. In task 5.4, students explore properties of the protractor and use it to measure angles. While students in grades 3–5 are likely to have many experiences using tools of linear measure, they probably have less or no familiarity with measuring angles. Task 5.5 engages students in the use of unit blocks as a measuring tool. In this task, students may employ different strategies to measure the volume of boxes. For example, students may fill a box with blocks and then count the blocks, or they may measure each dimension and then calculate volume using length × width × height. Task 5.5 allows students both to choose a method for themselves and also to discuss the use of other tools.

MP.7

"Look for and make use of structure" (NGA Center and CCSSO 2010, p. 7). In task 5.3, students explore the relationship between area and perimeter. In designing different gardens for Ethan, students may observe methods for determining the perimeter (or, the amount of fence in feet Ethan needs for a particular garden). They may notice that a perimeter of a rectangular garden (e.g., 6 × 4) resembles the calculation of perimeter for other rectangular gardens (e.g., 2 × 12) in that each dimension is added twice (e.g., 6 + 4 + 6 + 4,

92

or 6 × 2 + 4 × 2; and 2 + 12 + 2 + 12, or 2 × 2 + 12 × 2). Students may also observe that such a structure does not apply in the same way to non-rectangular gardens.

Representing and Interpreting Data

The Measurement and Data standards in grades 3–5 include representing and interpreting two kinds of data: categorical data and measurement data. The CCSSM standards for grade 3 emphasize understanding of both categorical and measurement data, while the standards for grades 4 and 5 highlight measurement data exclusively.

Representations of categorical data allow students to observe trends in their surrounding world. In particular, one grade 3 standard (3.MD.3) emphasizes the use of a picture graph and bar graph in addition to the use of non-unit scaling (e.g., a 2-to-1 scale in which two pets are represented by one unit in the representation, such as a picture of one cat representing two pets, or one square unit on grid paper representing two pets). In task 5.6, students represent the number of pets that children have in each grade, constructing a picture graph or bar graph as well as considering a 2-to-1 scale. This task allows them to build on their prior understandings involving categorical data to consider shifting scale, a mathematical property that will be a feature of mathematical representations across domains through grade 12.

Measurement data involve the use of a tool with standard units to measure the world around us. Unlike categorical data in which items often clearly fit a particular category (e.g., chocolate or vanilla ice cream), measurement data are subject to imprecision due to the use of measurement tools. In task 5.7, students use rulers to gather data in their own classrooms in order to construct a line plot. Data recorded on the line plot reveal the spread and variation across measurements taken by different groups, and this allows students to discuss trends in the data.

Task 5.6: How Many Pets?

At Chavez Elementary School, students collected data on how many pets students in each grade have. They found out that grade 1 students had 20 pets, grade 2 students had 8 pets, grade 3 students had 16 pets, and grade 4 students had 14 pets. Make a graph to show how many pets students in each grade have.

Launching the Task—Students should be familiar with the idea that many homes have pets, such as cats, dogs, or fish. Ask students about the pets they have at home or that friends or other families may have. Engage students in considering who has the most pets in the classroom. Indicate that they will represent some data about pets using a graph. Ask students to describe what they know about making graphs. They may indicate that bar graphs show you *how much* something is and allow for comparison of quantities, and they may state that they can use pictures of cats, fish, or other animals to represent each type of pet. To support students' access to the problem, consider drawing examples of a picture graph and a bar graph that can be used to represent the data on the board (or have one prepared). For example, consider introducing a character or someone you know who has four cats and two dogs. Guide a discussion in which these data are represented as a picture graph with a drawing of a cat representing each cat, and also as a bar graph.

Task Exploration—Present the problem to students. An alternative to this problem is to have students collect the data themselves in their own school. Such data collection supports scientific practices of inquiry and exploration, and it would provide students with authentic data to construct graphs (Curcio 2010). Instead of different grades, you may group data by classrooms at their grade level, or by table groups or sections of your classrooms. In any of these cases, some students may need organizational support to keep track of surveyed classmates, such as recording initials or using a roster. Post the problem on the board, or provide students with a half-sheet of paper on which the problem is stated. Provide students with grid and plain paper, and organize them into pairs or small groups to make a bar or picture graph. Depending on your students, you may wish to provide them with two axes to support access to the problem. To promote a discussion about scale for the summarizing discussion, indicate to students that they may create a bar graph in which each box (when using grid paper) represents two pets.

Summarizing Discussion—The final discussion involves both students sharing their representations of the data as well as a discussion about scale. First, have students share their different representations. You may organize students to do a gallery walk, or they may present their representations at the front of the classroom. If time is a concern, use informal observations during the task exploration to select a subset of groups to present their graphs so that the presentations reflect variety. Note in particular groups that used a scale in which one unit represented two pets.

After students have had the opportunity to present their graphs, ask the following:

- What was similar about these representations?
- What was different about these representations?

Students may notice that they can use the height of particular columns in the picture graph or bar graph to determine which grade level had the most and the fewest number of pets. They may also notice that some representations had pictures, whereas other representations had a solid bar.

If a group has scaled a graph differently, ask students about that particular graph. If no group has constructed a graph like this, introduce this during the final discussion. Teachers should note that this means that since you will need an example of a bar graph that uses a 2-to-1 scale for the summarizing discussion, you should have one prepared in the event that no students construct one during the task exploration. Support students by providing a legend that indicates that one box (or one cat picture or dog picture) represents two pets (see Curcio 2010). Engage students in considering the resulting graph, with comparison to a similar graph using unit scaling, through questions such as these:

- How are these graphs different?
- How can they represent the same data if they look so different?

The following task is adapted from one on pages 13–14 at http://commoncoretools .files.wordpress.com/2011/06/ccss_progression_md_k5_2011_06_20.pdf.

Task 5.7: Comparing Measurements

Use line plots to represent measurements of objects in your classroom. Record the height in centimeters of objects in the classroom. Using the measurement data for one of these objects, make a line plot to record the different measurements.

Launching the Task—Ask students to predict the measurement in centimeters of an object in the classroom, such as the edge of a table or the height of a bookcase. Indicate to them that today they will be measuring a series of objects in the classroom. Provide students with a list of objects to measure in centimeters. You may provide them with a table in which one column is a series of objects (e.g., the height of a bookcase, the length of a desk, the width of a textbook) and the next column provides a space for them to record the heights. Several columns should be available so that students can later record the measures of other groups (see table 5.3). As students record the different measures, observe their measurements. In particular, note objects that have variation across students' measurements. A wider (or taller, or higher) dimension is likely to have more variation than smaller objects. In order to engage students in considering fractions of a centimeter, ask them, how precise do you think you can be? Students may measure to the centimeter, half centimeter, quarter centimeter, or eighth of an centimeter.

Table 5.3
Example of part of a table to distribute to students

Object dimensions (in centimeters)	My group #_____	Group _____	Group _____	Group _____	Group _____	Group _____
Height of bookcase						
Width of textbook						
Width of teacher's desk						

Task Exploration—After students have had the opportunity to measure objects and record the results, indicate to them that you noticed varied measures for a particular object. Draw on the board (or have prepared ahead of time) a number line in order to begin a line plot. We advise using a number line that includes halves, fourths, and eighths (see fig. 5.8). Ask two or three pairs of students to share with you their data for a particular object, and begin to construct the line plot for them. Indicate to students that they will be making line plots of the measurement data they recorded.

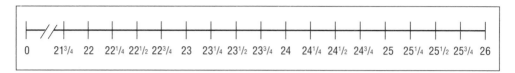

Fig. 5.8. Example of a line plot to provide to students

To do this, students will need the measurements of other groups in the classroom. Depending on time constraints, teachers may wish to choose a method to distribute this information. Student groups may read out the measurements for two or three objects as other groups record these on their sheets. Alternatively, you may provide students with a list of measurements that you indicate students in another classroom made for the same objects. For example, table 5.4 displays measurements that could be provided to students, allowing teachers to anticipate the structure of the summarizing discussion.

Table 5.4

Example of part of a table to provide to students

Group	Width of textbook (cm)
Group A	$23^3/_4$
Group B	$24^1/_2$
Group C	25
Group D	$23^1/_2$
Group E	24
Group F	$23^3/_4$
Group G	24
Group H	24
Group I	$24^1/_4$
Group J	$23^1/_4$
Group K	$23^1/_2$
Group L	$23^3/_4$
Group M	$23^3/_4$
Group N	$24^1/_4$
Group O	24

Table 5.4 Continued

Group	Width of textbook (cm)
Group P	$24^1/_4$
Group Q	$23^3/_4$
Group R	24
Group S	$23^1/_2$
Group T	$24^1/_4$
Group U	$24^1/_2$
Group V	24

Distribute to students number lines that are appropriate for the objects they measured. For example, for the measures provided in table 5.4, the number line should extend beyond the greatest measurement (see fig. 5.9). If using a number line representation with a break in it, draw attention to this before students begin representing data on the line plot. Ask questions such as these:

- What do you notice that is different about this number line?
- Why are there two diagonal lines in it?

Draw students' attention to the fact that there is a break in the line between 0 and $21^3/_4$. Next have students enter their data on the line plot, or provide a completed line plot such as the one in figure 5.9 that follows the data given in table 5.4.

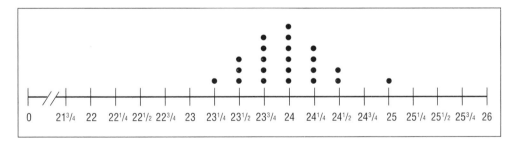

Fig. 5.9. The spread of data in the line plot

Summarizing Discussion—In the discussion, engage students in considering the overall data, and in particular the shape of the data. Consider asking questions such as the following:

- What is the difference between the greatest measure and the least measure? How do you know?
- What do you notice about the shape of the data?

- What do you notice about the values that most students found? Where are those on the line plot?

- What do you notice about the values that not many students found? Where are those on the line plot?

- What would a student from another class think the height of the bookcase is using this line plot? Why do you think that?

- Could we have measured more precisely? For example, between $23^3/_4$ and 24?

Use these or other questions to engage students in considering the spread of the data, shown in figure 5.9. The final question reflects that linear measure is continuous and that, with the appropriate measuring tool, students may have found a height that falls somewhere between the values provided on the line.

STANDARDS *for Mathematical Practice—Tasks 5.6 and 5.7*

MP.4

"Model with mathematics" (NGA Center and CCSSO 2010, p. 7). CCSSM underscores the use of mathematics to represent phenomena arising in everyday life. Task 5.7 engages students in representing measurement data in a line plot. Such a representation involves students in a model of mathematical properties of objects in the world around them.

MP.6

"Attend to precision" (NGA Center and CCSSO 2010, p. 7). Tasks 5.6 and 5.7 reflect attention to precision in different ways. In task 5.6, students use a picture or bar graph to explore issues of scale. Scale is a concept that will continue to weave through different mathematical topics through high school and beyond. Task 5.6 engages students in considering a non-unit scale, a critical skill for students to develop that will support their construction and interpretation of mathematical representations. In task 5.7, a line plot is used to represent measurement data. The line plot draws attention to the challenge of precision in measurement, and it engages students in considering how trends in the line plot indicate which measurements are more or less likely to be precise.

MP7

"Look for and make use of repeated structure" (NGA Center and CCSSO 2010, p. 8). Graphical representations such as those in tasks 5.6 and 5.7 allow individuals to consider overall trends in a body of data, thereby supporting an analysis of the mathematical structure. In the non-unit graph in task 5.6, students coordinate scale on a vertical axis with each bar in order to determine quantity. Such a task supports students' analytic skills in interpreting a ratio scale. The line plot of task 5.7 supports an analysis of data trends—in this case, of a set of measurements.

Chapter 6
Geometry

The word *geometry* is composed of two Greek root words: *geo*, meaning "earth," and *metria*, which means "to measure." In discussions of the history and origins of geometry, the general understanding is that the study of geometry was prevalent in many ancient civilizations. Geometry as we now think about it, however, with an emphasis on reasoning and proofs, was made famous by the Greek mathematician Euclid.

From an instructional perspective, geometry provides opportunities for connections to be made within and across the various domains of the Common Core State Standards for Mathematics (CCSSM). For example, the connection between measurement and geometry is explicitly addressed in CCSSM under the measurement section. When exploring shapes and lines of symmetry, students have the opportunity to make connections to fractions, as we see in task 4.3 in chapter 4, Number and Operations—Fractions. Furthermore, the emphasis on reasoning with shapes and their attributes can be a bridge to algebraic thinking when attention is drawn to general properties that distinguish categories of shapes from each other. Teachers are encouraged to take advantage of geometry as a natural visual platform for integrating the curriculum across CCSSM domains.

In this chapter, we base our discussion on how to support problem solving in geometry by integrating the use of manipulatives, visual representations, and numeric notation to support students in reasoning and providing justification for their reasoning. At each grade level for grades 3–5, the Common Core includes a set of standards that are clustered or grouped together to facilitate teachers working to support their students in making mathematical connections. One approach to teaching geometry would be to attend to specific grade levels and find tasks that address the clusters and standards *within* each grade level. Here, we take an *across*-grade-level perspective similar to other chapters in this volume, because we believe that it is natural to encounter a range among students within a particular class. We offer various strategies for teachers to differentiate instruction. As we note in previous chapters, this across-grade-level organization can also be helpful for teachers who have multiage or multigrade teaching assignments.

The appendix provides a progression of the standards across grade levels. In the previous grade band, kindergarten–grade 2, geometry standards serve two different functions in anticipation of grades 3–5: (*a*) to prepare students for fractions when they get to grade 3, and (*b*) to begin to engage students with identification, analysis, and reasoning with shapes. In grades 3–5, the reasoning and analysis component is further developed (e.g., an examination of the similarities and differences between a rectangle, square, and rhombus). Furthermore, there is a distinct focus on *geometric measurement*, the standards for which are outlined under the topic of measurement and may be found in chapter 5. Moreover, in grade 5, students are introduced to beginning concepts of coordinate geometry. These concepts include naming axes and locating ordered pairs on coordinate planes, solving real-world and mathematical problems involving graphing points in the first quadrant, and interpreting coordinate points in the context of particular situations. In grades 6–8, students continue to delve deeper into all of the areas developed in grades 3–5, with an additional emphasis on being able to provide informal lines of argumentation and understanding as well as understanding and applying the Pythagorean theorem. Geometry is a standard that covers all grades from kindergarten to grade 12.

In elementary school, there are several big ideas that teachers can focus on when planning instruction in geometry. First, *geometric properties*—e.g., number of lines, angles, parallel or perpendicular lines, lines of symmetry, and congruence—can be used to determine how shapes are alike and different. These properties can in turn be used to understand how different shapes such as rhombuses, rectangles, or squares (to name a few) can fall into a larger category such as quadrilaterals. Second, viewing shapes from different *perspectives* allows us to see the relationship between two and three-dimensional figures. Third, *coordinate systems* can be used to describe the location of shapes in planes or in space. In organizing the standards across grade levels, we identify three distinct areas that need attention when teaching geometry in grades 3–5. These three areas are:

(1) Classifying and reasoning with shapes and their attributes,

(2) Drawing and identifying lines and angles, and classifying shapes based on properties of their lines and angles, and

(3) Understanding coordinate geometry.

What follows are tasks that can support classifying and reasoning with shapes and their attributes (tasks 6.1, 6.2, and 6.3), drawing and identifying lines and angles and classifying shapes based on properties of their lines and angles (task 6.4), and understanding coordinate geometry (tasks 6.5 and 6.6).

Table 6.1 provides a reference for content area, tasks, content standards, and mathematical practices. While we target particular content standards for each task, the tasks may be extended to address other standards in the domain of geometry.

The tasks presented in this chapter demonstrate how different mathematical practices can be at play during the different phases of the task. These tasks provide connections to many of the Common Core Standards for Mathematical Practice. It is worth noting that in grades 3–5, the content standards in the domain of geometry focus on visualization. The standards for geometric measurement in chapter 5 provide opportunities for abstract and quantitative thinking in the context of geometry, thus addressing MP.2. The connections that we see between the tasks and mathematical practices are by no means exhaustive and as teachers modify the tasks based on their needs, they will make connections to other mathematical practices.

One common framework present in discussions of how to differentiate instruction when planning instruction in geometry is the van Hiele Levels of Geometric Thought. This framework delineates a five-level hierarchy of how to understand the development of geometric thinking: (*a*) visualization, (*b*) analysis, (*c*) informal deduction, (*d*) deduction, and (*e*) rigor. If teachers are drawing on other instructional resources in geometry that are developed based on the van Hiele Levels, it will be more productive to focus on how specific tasks can spur specific types of geometric thinking—visualization, analysis, and so on, instead of trying to categorize into which level of geometric thinking their students fall.

Table 6.1
Content areas, grade-level standards, and mathematical practice standards met by the tasks in chapter 6

Content Areas	Tasks	Grade 3 Standards	Grade 4 Standards	Grade 5 Standards	Standards for Mathematical Practice
Classifying and reasoning with shapes and their attributes	6.1	3.G.1	4.G.2	5.G.3 5.G.4	MP.5, MP.6
	6.2		4.G.3		
Drawing and identifying lines and angles and classifying shapes based on properties of their lines and angles	6.3		4.G.1 4.G.2		MP.3, MP.4, MP.7
Understanding coordinate geometry	6.4			5.G.1 5.G.2	MP.3
	6.5			5.G.1 5.G.2	

Classifying and Reasoning with Shapes and Their Attributes

A key advantage of having children reason with shapes and attributes is that it helps them understand when to focus on specific shapes, such as rectangles or rhombuses, and when to entertain a larger category such as quadrilaterals (see fig. 6.1).

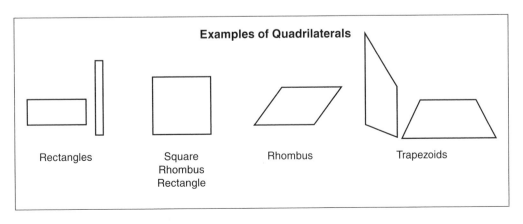

Fig. 6.1. Examples of quadrilaterals

It can also help students understand that geometric properties such as numbers of sides, angles, or types of lines (e.g., parallel or perpendicular) can be used as resources for justifying their reasoning. A focus on categorizing and classifying based on the attributes and properties of shapes is present throughout grades 3–5. One of the standards under the grade 3 cluster of "reason[ing] with shapes and their attributes," standard 3.G.2, involves partitioning shapes into parts with equal areas and expressing the area of each part as a unit fraction (National Governors Association Center for Best Practices and Council of Chief State School Officers [NGA Center and CCSSO] 2010, p. 26). This standard has significant overlap with standard 3.NF.1 in the fractions domain. In chapter 4, task 4.3 addresses standard 3.G.2 as well.

Shape riddles can be an excellent way to help students focus on properties and attributes of shapes and develop the understanding that, depending on the properties in question, shapes may shift from one category to another. Task 6.1 is a set of such riddles that is a modified version of one from Van de Walle, Karp, and Bay-Williams (2010). In grade 3, engaging in the activity in this task can specifically support standard 3.G.1. This standard involves understanding that shapes in different categories such as rhombuses, rectangles, squares, and trapezoids can be grouped together because they all have four sides, putting them in the category of "quadrilaterals." In grade 4, shape riddles can support standard 4.G.2, classifying two-dimensional figures based on the presence or absence of parallel and perpendicular lines or the presence or absence of particular types of angles, and recognizing right triangles as a particular category (task 6.1.V).

In grade 5, shape riddles (tasks 6.1.II and 6.1.III) are a good activity to support the development of the concept of categories and subcategories of shapes (5.G.3) and their corresponding hierarchy (5.G.4). Figure 6.2 shows one way the hierarchy of shapes can be represented. While most students will have had intuitive experience with "open" and "closed" shapes, it is always helpful for students to connect them in relation to one another.

Analyzing and classifying two-dimensional figures in relation to the term *hierarchy* is an explicit focus in grade 5 (5.G.3; 5.G.4). Prior to grade 5, the standards call for students to make connections among particular categories and subcategories within the hierarchy. For example, in grade 3, standard 3.G.1 focuses on quadrilaterals as a category. Within that standard, the expectation is that students will be able to "recognize rhombuses, rectangles, and squares as examples of quadrilaterals, and draw examples of quadrilaterals that do not belong to any of these subcategories" (NGA Center and CCSSO 2010, p. 26). Developing a hierarchical perspective prepares students for geometry in middle school, especially in grade 6, where students have to find the areas of triangles by composing or decomposing rectangles or other quadrilaterals. For example, an equilateral triangle can be extended to form a rhombus whose area is double that of the equilateral triangle, while the area of the equilateral triangle is half that of the rhombus (see fig. 6.3).

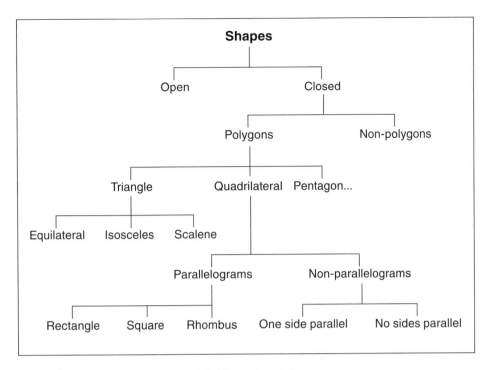

Fig. 6.2. Hierarchy of shapes

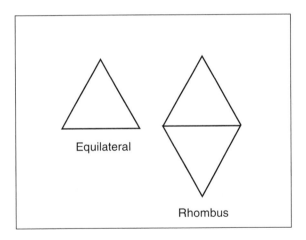

Fig. 6.3. Relationship of equilateral triangle and rhombus

When teachers are engaging students in the Shape Riddles activity in grade 5, they can introduce the hierarchy presented in figure 6.2 during the summarizing discussion. Standard 4.G.3, recognizing and identifying lines of symmetry, can also be taught in an integrated fashion, drawing on other properties such as congruence (see task 6.2).

Task 6.1: Shape Riddles

The following questions relate to the set of quadrilaterals shown in figure 6.4:

(I)   I am a quadrilateral but I am not a square. Which of the shapes (*a–i*) could I be? How do you know? Explain.

(II) I am a quadrilateral but I am not a square, or a rectangle, or a rhombus, or a parallelogram. Which of the shapes (*a–i*) could I be? How do you know? Explain.

(III) I am a quadrilateral but I am not a parallelogram. Which of the shapes (*a–i*) could I be? How do you know? Explain.

(IV) I am a quadrilateral and I have four right angles. Which of the shapes (*a–i*) could I be? How do you know? Explain.

(V)   I am a quadrilateral and I have no right angles. Which of the shapes (*a–i*) could I be? How do you know? Explain.

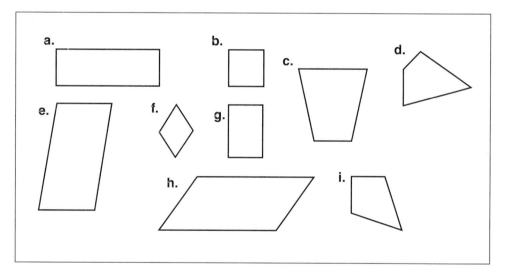

Fig. 6.4. Set of quadrilateral shapes

Launching the Task—The task can be launched in various ways. Students may be more successful with this task if teachers use some concrete visuals such as a bag of everyday shapes or sets of cutout shapes (see fig. 6.4) so that students can use them to reason about shapes and their attributes. This task also provides an excellent opportunity for teachers to help students develop academic mathematics vocabulary while simultaneously attending to English language development. Depending on the group of students, teachers may choose to include in the task sets of closed shapes that have straight and curved lines such as those in figure 6.5 in order to have whole-class discussions that help students focus on properties of shapes. This might help students with their justifications when working on this task.

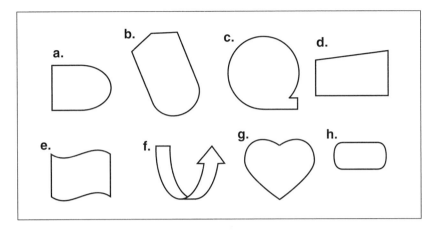

Fig. 6.5. Closed shapes with straight and curved lines

One suggested way to launch the task is to use a whole-group discussion in which teachers ask students to select one shape and then tell the rest of the class about one or two properties of the shape they find interesting. To follow up, two different students could each pick a shape at random, and the class could brainstorm the properties that are alike and different between the two shapes. The teacher could also select a shape from the set and display it as the *target shape.* A discussion could then center on students selecting other shapes and providing a justification for why their selected shape belongs in the same category as the target shape. For example, this shape is the same as the target shape because it has a curved line and a straight line. Teachers will note that in the set of shapes in figure 6.5 there are several shapes (that is, *d, e,* and *h*) that are specifically included to focus discussion on particularities of quadrilaterals since task 6.1 is geared toward quadrilaterals.

If you feel that your students might need additional support in conceptual development before engaging in task 6.1, see the "Additional Activities" section below, which includes two added suggestions for engaging students with quadrilaterals. Teachers may wish to use those ideas in order to launch this task, or as a re-teaching resource after completing the task.

Task Exploration—The entire task can be presented on one handout, or each riddle can be presented on a note card. Presenting the riddles using note cards will facilitate time management for the lesson. For example, by using note cards the teacher does not have to wait for each student to be finished with every riddle. The class will be ready for discussion as soon as all riddles have been solved. On the other hand, if each student works on all the riddles, that will support a more engaged and knowledgeable discussion since everyone will have had an opportunity to grapple with each riddle. Teachers should feel free to organize the flow so that it suits their instructional objective. As students start exploring the set of quadrilaterals in pairs or small groups, teachers are encouraged to walk around and listen to students' conversations and assist students as needed. If students need support getting started, help them to focus on the properties of particular classes of shapes that they are asked to consider in each subsection of the shape riddle. For example, in task 6.1.I, students have to identify a shape that is a quadrilateral but not a square. In this case, teachers might encourage students to make a list of the attributes that make a quadrilateral and those that make a square in order to scaffold their identifying a shape from the set that is a quadrilateral but is not a square. As teachers walk around, they will find that there are students who may be able to solve the shape riddles but are having a hard time justifying their answer. A similar strategy of asking students to create a written list of attributes of both classes of shapes being compared will assist students in making evidence-based justifications.

Summarizing Discussion—Once all students have had an opportunity to explore the shape riddles, the class should come together for a whole-group discussion. Students should be encouraged to share the strategies they used to compare the different shapes. Teachers can model how students might generate property lists for categories of shapes and how they might use the property lists to solve the riddles. Some suggested questions for discussion are:

- What was your strategy for solving the shape riddles?
- What properties must be present for a shape to be categorized as a quadrilateral?
- What properties must be present for a shape to be categorized as a square?
- How are non-square quadrilaterals and squares similar? How are they different?
- How can you use these property lists to help you solve the riddles?

Adapting for Grade 5—The focus on quadrilaterals when playing shape riddles is more geared to grade 3 (3.G.1). To adapt it for grade 5 (5.G.3), teachers may refer to the hierarchy in figure 6.2 and add clues for other shapes that might include open shapes as well.

Additional Activities—During the lesson, if the teacher finds that students are having difficulty in coordinating how to generate property lists and compare them, teachers can engage them in this follow-up activity described below and return to the Shape Riddles task using a different set of quadrilaterals.

First, provide a group of three to four students with a set of different shapes that belong to the same category (see fig. 6.6) and ask them to generate a **Property List for Quadrilaterals.**

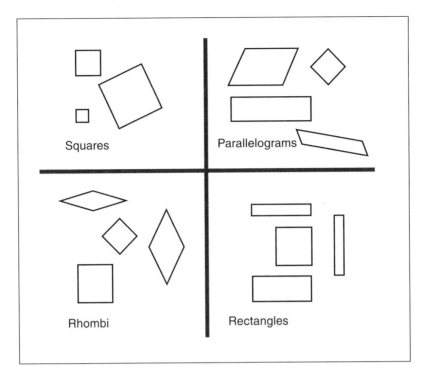

Fig. 6.6. Shapes for the Property List of Quadrilaterals activity

Ask students to analyze their set of shapes under the following headings: *sides, parallel lines, angles,* and *symmetry.* In grade 3, students might be asked to focus only on *sides* and *parallel lines.* Teachers may use this opportunity to introduce other properties, such as *angles* and *symmetry,* that students will encounter in grades 4 and 5.

A second follow-up activity is creating **Minimal Defining Lists** (MDL). (This activity is also modified from one in Van de Walle, Karp, and Bay-Williams 2010.) If students need further assistance in making connections across categories of shapes and developing the ability to reason from an "if-then" perspective to support *informal deduction* (as it is described by level 2 of the van Hiele hierarchy), MDL can be an excellent activity. MDL helps students to focus on specific conditions that define a particular category of shape. For example, the MDL for a square is that it (*a*) is a closed shape, (*b*) is a quadrilateral, (*c*) has sides of the same length, and (*d*) has all right angles. If we were to remove any one of these conditions, we would no longer be defining a square. We recommend that the MDL activity be done after students have had a chance to do the previous activity of generating property lists for quadrilaterals. Once property lists for different categories of shapes have been generated (and perhaps posted visibly around the class), students can be asked to discuss and generate minimal defining lists and share their responses in the whole group.

Task 6.2: Twin Shapes

Alex and Aya are at school exploring shapes. Their teacher wants them to figure out a way to make the kite below into two smaller congruent shapes, or *twin shapes,* using a *line of symmetry.* The dotted line in figure 6.7 shows where Alex and Aya drew a line of symmetry.

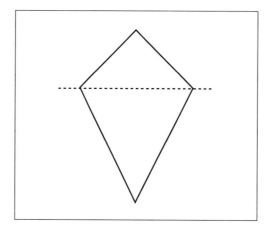

Fig. 6.7. Alex and Aya's line of symmetry

(*a*) Do you agree that the line they drew is a line of symmetry? If so, why?

If you don't, where would you draw a line of symmetry to divide the kite into twin shapes?

(*b*) Explain using words and drawings why you are sure that the line you have drawn is a line of symmetry.

Launching the Task—Teachers may wish to begin with a discussion of the concept of *congruence.* They may ask students to consider congruence in terms of their own body parts, everyday shapes and objects drawn from the classroom, or through use of manipulatives such as pattern blocks.

To transition to the concept of congruence in relation to symmetry (4.G.3), it is recommended that teachers structure the next phase of the discussion using *one* shape. Giving students a paper shape, such as a square, that they can manipulate (fold or cut) along different dimensions (vertically, horizontally, or diagonally) assists students with understanding that the same shape can be manipulated in different ways to create two smaller "twin shapes." Depending on the circumstances, these discussions can happen in the context of another content area such as art or English language development.

Task Exploration—To prepare for the task exploration phase, teachers should prepare multiple cutouts of the kite for students to manipulate. Teachers should also ensure that all students know what the task is asking them to do. It is helpful to stress to students that it is not enough to take a position about whether or not they agree. They are also required to justify their position when working in pairs and presenting their thinking to the whole group. During the exploration phase, students will benefit from the opportunity to think about the task individually before they engage in discussions about it in small groups or with a partner. As they work individually, teachers should walk around, listen to students, and provide assistance as appropriate. Many students may use the folding approach and decide that Alex and Aya's solution is incorrect. Teachers can remind those students to work on how to help Alex and Aya with their problem and come up with justifications that will demonstrate that their solution to the line of symmetry is correct.

Summarizing Discussion—After the task exploration, students should engage as a whole class in a summarizing discussion focused on whether Alex and Aya had indeed drawn the line of symmetry correctly to form two twin shapes. Some questions that may be helpful in guiding that discussion are presented below. The last two bulleted items addressing area and perimeter provide examples of how we can connect to the Measurement and Data domain of the Common Core. In those same bulleted items, the accompanying question of whether or not the relationship in question holds true for "all" kites is an underlying bridge to algebraic thinking, as it draws attention to general properties of any kite.

- What strategies did you use to figure out whether the line that Alex and Aya drew was indeed a "line of symmetry"?
- Does this kite have more than one line of symmetry?
- Are there any other pairs of twin shapes that can be made by cutting this kite in another way?
- What can you predict about the relationship between the areas of the twin shapes made from decomposing the kite? Will the relationship between the areas of the twin shapes be true of all twin shapes made by decomposing kites?
- What can you predict about the relationship between the perimeters of the twin shapes made from decomposing the kite? Will the relationship between the perimeters of the twin shapes be true of all twin shapes made by decomposing kites?

STANDARDS *for Mathematical Practice—Tasks 6.1 and 6.2*

MP.5

"Use appropriate tools strategically" is the fifth Standard for Mathematical Practice (NGA Center and CCSSO 2010, p. 7). As it is stated in the description of this standard, "Proficient students are sufficiently familiar with tools appropriate for their grade or course to make sound decisions about when each of these tools might be helpful" (NGA Center and CCSSO 2010, p. 7). Tools are likely to be employed during the task exploration portion of the lesson and can include physical tools (such as manipulatives), semantic tools (such as lists), and graphic organizers as in the tasks discussed above. Students, however, can only use tools that they are familiar with and have on hand. For tasks 6.1 and 6.2, it may be necessary for the teacher to introduce how to use lists or graphic organizers or how to take notes on a note card; in that way, such tools will be helpful to students for supporting their justifications during the summarizing discussion.

MP.6

"Attend to precision" (NGA Center and CCSSO 2010, p. 7). This sixth practice is at play during the launch and task exploration phases of these tasks. In both instances, students are expected to "communicate ideas precisely," as they explain and provide justifications (NGA Center and CCSSO 2010, p. 7). Another important point regarding precision is a focus on vocabulary, which is a primary component of both task 6.1 and task 6.2. A third point of attention is the mathematical definitions that are pertinent to working on a particular problem. Both tasks presented above require students to attend to mathematical definitions.

Drawing and Identifying Lines and Angles and Classifying Shapes

As students move through the Geometry domain in grades 3–5, it is in grade 4 where they will meet an explicit focus on drawing and identifying lines and angles and on classifying shapes based on those properties (4.G.1, 4.G.2). Task 6.3, which engages students in this focus, is modified from an activity by Marilyn Burns (2000).

Task 6.3: Categorizing Letters of the Alphabet

Analyze the capital letters on the alphabet chart. With your partner, decide which letters of the alphabet fall into the categories listed below. Letters can fall into more than one category. Clearly label and explain how you see the match between the category and each letter of the alphabet.

  (1) Letters that have parallel line segments
  (2) Letters that have perpendicular line segments
  (3) Letters that have both parallel and perpendicular line segments
  (4) Letters that have acute angles
  (5) Letters that have obtuse angles
  (6) Letters that have straight angles

(7) Letters that feature a right angle

(8) Letter that have no perpendicular lines, parallel lines, or angles

Launching the Task—Before launching the task, it is recommended that teachers review the definitions and concepts students will be drawing upon. If this is the first time students are being introduced to these concepts, teachers may introduce two or three letters of the alphabet (e.g., *E, F,* and *L*) to discuss the characteristics, likenesses, and differences among them. In this way the teacher can introduce terms such as *parallel, perpendicular,* and *right angle.* Other letters of the alphabet can be strategically chosen to introduce acute and obtuse angles. In grades 4 and 5, teachers may even introduce using protractors in this discussion to help students connect tools for measuring two-dimensional shapes. (Note that students are not required to construct shapes formally using geometric tools like protractors until grade 7.) Easily accessible visuals of the different types of lines and angles, which might be arranged on a chart, can greatly assist students in focusing on the task because less energy will be expended on recalling definitions. A note card can often be a good manipulative to use to make concrete connections with concepts such as parallel lines, perpendicular lines, right angles, and others.

Task Exploration—Teachers may have students start off working in pairs, or else begin working individually and then come together with partners. If students need assistance in making the connections, teachers might encourage students to refer to definitions, visuals, or manipulatives (such as the note card). If students have been introduced to graphic organizers such as tree maps or Venn diagrams, teachers may encourage students to use those to help them track letters of the alphabet in overlapping categories.

Summarizing Discussion—The main emphasis of this cluster of standards in grade 4 is to help students develop some familiarity with the basic terms in geometry they will draw upon in subsequent grades as they start working with coordinate geometry, reasoning, and proof. Given this specific lens, the emphasis of the discussion questions can be more about their observations regarding the letters of the alphabet. Some suggested questions are:

- Which category had the most letters of the alphabet?
- Which category had the fewest letters of the alphabet?
- Were some letters of the alphabet harder to categorize than others? Which ones? Why?
- Did you make any interesting observations about the letters of the alphabet?

Additional Activity—Teachers who would like to provide students more opportunity to apply these terms and concepts (instead of simply "identifying" and "recognizing" them) may give students the following activity:

Here's how to play **Guess My Letter of the Alphabet.** First, select a letter of the alphabet that you want to work with. Using geometric vocabulary such as *parallel lines, perpendicular lines, acute angles,* and so forth, write a description of that letter. When you have finished writing your description of one letter, choose another. Continue in this way until you are asked to move to work with a partner. At this point, you will read your partner the description of one of your letters. Your partner will have to figure out which letter of the alphabet you are describing. Then switch roles! Continue like this until you each have had the opportunity to present the descriptions of all your letters.

STANDARDS *for Mathematical Practice—Task 6.3*

MP.3

"Construct viable arguments and critique the reasoning of others" (NGA Center and CCSSO 2010, p. 6). As students engage in categorizing letters of the alphabet, the *exploration* and *discussion* portions of the lesson provide opportunities for students to construct arguments about their categorization. It is important for teachers to remember that for elementary school students, even in grades 3–5, it is common to construct arguments through the use of concrete materials including drawings. If students have no opportunity to listen and respond to the reasoning of other students, it is unlikely that they will be able to meet this standard.

MP.4

"Model with mathematics" (NGA Center and CCSSO 2010, p. 7). In task 6.3, students are modeling with mathematics as they use letters of the alphabet to make a tangible connection to angles. This modeling occurs during the task exploration and discussion phases of the lesson.

MP.7

"Look for and make use of structure" (NGA Center and CCSSO 2010, p. 8). As students work on categorizing the letters of the alphabet, they will notice patterns or structure. When they are working on a task during the task exploration phase, these observations can be elicited with questioning and probing by the teacher as she interacts with them. The teacher can also highlight aspects of patterns or structures that occur within the mathematical task during the discussion phase. In this way, students' attention can be drawn to these features of the task and their growing understandings can be supported.

Coordinate Geometry

Coordinate geometry is introduced in grade 5. The main objective of this cluster of standards is to introduce students to another representational tool to describe locations in space, one that will gain in importance as a representation in middle school and high school. In grade 5, the focus is on students becoming familiar with the coordinate system, using the x and y axes, understanding that the origin—that is, $(0, 0)$—is where the axes intersect, being able to locate a point on the plane given its coordinates, and interpreting coordinate values of points in the context of a real-life situation such as orienteering. This prepares students for geometry in middle school where they will further explore properties of shapes, learn about transformations (i.e., changes in position), and use the coordinate grid in conjunction with the Pythagorean theorem to solve real-world problems.

Task 6.4 (Watch the Scale!) is an excellent task to help students understand some of the norms and conventions of labeling axes and the impact that has on how location is read or represented in space. Task 6.5 addresses most aspects of standard 5.G.1, on how to draw and name axes and how to represent the origin and ordered pairs on the grid. It also addresses standard 5.G.2, interpreting coordinate values in the context of a particular situation. In this case, the context is the scale's unit on the grid.

Mystery Polygons (task 6.5) also provides students with an opportunity to explore the coordinate grid, but it does so in the context of a collection of ordered pairs that produce polygons when joined together. This task also addresses standards 5.G.1 and 5.G.2, and it can assist students in understanding the relationship between scale and size.

The following task is adapted from Earnest (2012, p. 12).

Task 6.4: Watch the Scale!

On a test, Michael's teacher asked him to write out the coordinates of the point on a graph that she gave him (see fig. 6.8). Michael labeled the point as (3.5, 3.5). When he got the test back, he was surprised to see that he got the problem wrong and that the correct coordinates were (5, 5). Can you help him understand what happened? What should he do differently the next time?

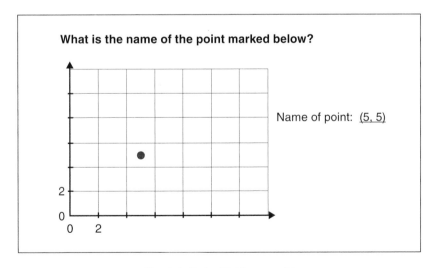

Fig. 6.8. Point (5, 5) on a grid

Note: It is not unusual for students to arrive at a response of (3.5, 3.5) for the point on the grid by starting at the points on the *x*- and *y*-axes labeled "2" and then counting subsequent increments by one. Another common misconception is to treat each increment as having a value of "1," thus arriving at a response of (2.5, 2.5) for the point on the grid.

Launching the Task—The main objective of this task is to highlight for students some basic aspects of the coordinate system that they should focus on such as (*a*) scale, (*b*) representing coordinates correctly in relation to the *x*- and *y*-axes, and (*c*) changes in the location of an ordered pair based on scale. Research on student thinking demonstrates that often students assume that the scale is a one-unit scale and represent the ordered pair according to that assumption.

Before presenting the task, teachers may choose to play a game that is similar to a "battleship" game in which pairs of students play with each other to guess positions of hidden objects on their game boards. Various versions of this game are available as board games and also available online (e.g., see http://www.learn4good.com/games/board/battleship.htm). The game allows students to think about identifying location using two referent points. Once students start thinking about location from this perspective, they can be introduced to the conventions of how to locate points on quadrant I of the coordinate grid. To give students more opportunities to practice working with the coordinate grid, teachers can ask them to execute a simple line drawing on graph paper and then to generate a list of ordered pairs that would allow a partner to reproduce their drawing. If the figure the partner constructs from the list of ordered pairs is identical to the original line drawing, then we know that there was success in reading, communicating, and locating the ordered pairs. After these initial discussions, present students with task 6.4.

Task Exploration—After students have had an opportunity to work on the task individually, teachers may have them discuss in pairs what they think about Michael's response. While students are discussing the task, it is recommended that the teacher walk around and listen to students' conversations. If the teacher notices that students are confused—that is, if students think Michael's answer was correct because, like Michael, they are not attending to the unit of the scale—he or she could point students to the numeric values and ask them where they might place 1, 3, 5 according to that scale. If students are having a hard time responding to those questions, teachers may ask students to redraw the coordinate graph and place (5, 5) on that. Often the act of reconstructing the coordinate grid, labeling the grid, and so on spurs students to notice that the scale in the task is a two-unit scale.

Summarizing Discussion—Once students have had an opportunity to develop a rationale, they can come together for a whole-class discussion. The following are some suggested questions for the discussion:

- Do you agree with what Michael identified as the ordered pair? Why or why not?
- Can you explain to Michael what he should do the next time so he does not make the same mistake?

- How would the ordered pair be different if the coordinate grid was constructed in one-unit intervals? Four-unit intervals?

Task 6.5: Mystery Polygons

The coordinates in figure 6.9 are clues to make three different mystery polygons. Use the graph paper you are given to graph the coordinates and construct the polygons. Once you are done, look around. You will find that some of your classmates have the same shapes but in different sizes. Why do you think that is? Turn your graph paper over and explain why you think people have different-sized shapes when everyone used the same coordinates.

(x, y)	(x, y)	(x, y)
(10, 10)	(1, 16)	(18, 5)
(13, 15)	(7, 16)	(16, 7)
(16, 10)	(9, 19)	(14, 7)
(10, 10)	(3, 19)	(12, 5)
	(1, 16)	(12, 3)
		(14, 1)
		(16, 1)
		(18, 3)
		(18, 5)

Fig. 6.9. Sets of coordinate points to use in constructing mystery polygons

Note: Teachers will need to prepare coordinate grids such that in some cases a one-point scale is used, while in other cases a two-point scale is employed. It is recommended that only one- or two- point scales be used, as this will reduce confusion and greatly assist discussion in the summarizing phase.

Launching the Task—This task addresses the same standards as task 6.5 and includes the added dimension of examining the impact of scale on the size of objects. Depending on the class, teachers may use task 6.5 as a review of concepts and this task as an assessment of the extent to which students are attending to issues of scale. To launch the task, teachers can provide students with the coordinates of the mystery polygons (see fig. 6.9) and ask students to make predictions about what the polygons might be based on the list of ordered pairs. Teachers should ensure that all students know what "one-point" and "two-point" scales mean, as that is one of the key aspects of being able to engage in discussions about the problem. Depending on their students, teachers may either ask students to work on all three polygons or select any one of them.

Task Exploration—As students start working on constructing the polygons, teachers may walk around and observe how students are locating the points. Students sometimes get confused between the *x*- and *y*-coordinates. Once students are finished, the teacher may want to group students strategically and encourage them to make observations of each other's work. Teachers might group students according to those who have constructed the same polygons and then ask students to discuss what might be causing the differences in size. Teachers might want to regroup students, this time based on students who used one- versus two-unit interval scales and ask them to talk to each other. Students will probably note that all of the shapes drawn on a grid with one-unit intervals are smaller than the shapes drawn on grids with two-unit intervals. Teachers might provide students with note cards to write down their observations from the small-group discussion so that they can refer to them during the whole-class discussion.

Summarizing Discussion—During the whole-group discussion, teachers can ask students to share the observations they made during individual and group explorations. The main objective is to guide the discussion such that students understand the relationship between scale and size. The following are suggested questions for doing this:

- What did you notice about the polygons?
- What do you think was impacting the size of the polygons?
- How would a 3-point scale impact the size of the polygon?
- Does a bigger scale always mean bigger size?
- What other factors might impact size?
- What connections are there between the number of ordered pairs and the number of sides of the polygons?

STANDARDS *for Mathematical Practice—Tasks 6.4 and 6.5*

MP.3

"Construct viable arguments and critique reasoning of others" (NGA Center and CCSSO 2010, p. 6). In both tasks discussed in this section, students have an opportunity to construct arguments that support their thinking about the problem. Both tasks require students to create viable arguments to unpack issues related to scale. In task 6.4, students have to provide a convincing argument to Michael, the student referenced in the task, as they critique his work. In task 6.5, students have to construct justifications that make connections to size of scale and size of object (i.e., using a larger scale will magnify an object and vice versa).

Appendix

CCSS Overview for Mathematics in Kindergarten through Grade 5

Grade Level	Content				
	Counting and Cardinality	Operations and Algebraic Thinking	Number and Operations in Base Ten	Measurement and Data	Geometry
Kindergarten	• Know number names and the count sequence. • Count to tell the number of objects. • Compare numbers.	• Understand addition as putting together and adding to. • Understand subtraction as taking apart and taking from.	• Work with numbers 11–19 to gain foundations for place value.	• Describe and compare measurable attributes. • Classify objects and count the number of objects in categories.	• Identify and describe shapes. • Analyze, compare, create, and compose shapes.
Grade 1		• Represent and solve problems involving addition and subtraction. • Understand and apply the properties of operations and the relationship between addition and subtraction. • Add and subtract within 20. • Work with addition and subtraction equations.	• Extend the counting sequence. • Understand place value. • Use place-value understanding and the properties of operations to add and subtract.	• Measure lengths indirectly and by iterating length units. • Tell and write time. • Represent and interpret data.	• Reason with shapes and their attributes.
Grade 2		• Represent and solve problems involving addition and subtraction. • Add and subtract within 20. • Work with equal groups of objects to gain foundations for multiplication.	• Understand place value. • Use place-value understanding and the properties of operations to add and subtract.	• Measure and estimate lengths in standard units. • Relate addition and subtraction to length. • Work with time and money. • Represent and interpret data.	• Reason with shapes and their attributes.

Grade Level	Content				
	Operations and Algebraic Thinking	Number and Operations in Base Ten	Number and Operations—Fractions	Measurement and Data	Geometry
Grade 3	• Represent and solve problems involving multiplication and division. • Understand the properties of multiplication and the relationship between multiplication and division. • Multiply and divide within 100. • Solve problems involving the four operations, and identify and explain patterns in arithmetic.	• Use place-value understanding and the properties of operations to perform multi-digit arithmetic.	• Develop understanding of fractions as numbers.	• Represent and interpret data.	• Reason with shapes and their attributes.
Grade 4	• Use the four operations with whole numbers to solve problems. • Gain familiarity with factors and multiples. • Generate and analyze patterns.	• Generalize place-value understanding for multi-digit whole numbers. • Use place-value understanding and properties of operations to perform multi-digit arithmetic.	• Extend understanding of fraction equivalence and ordering. • Build fractions from unit fractions by applying and extending previous understanding of operations on whole numbers. • Understand decimal notation for fractions, and compare decimal fractions.	• Solve problems involving measurement and conversion of measurements from a larger unit to a smaller unit. • Represent and interpret data. • Geometric measurement: understand concepts of angle and measure angles.	• Draw and identify lines and angles, and classify shapes by properties of their lines and angles.

	Content			
Grade Level	**Operations and Algebraic Thinking**	**Number and Operations in Base Ten**	**Number and Operations— Fractions**	**Measurement and Data**	**Geometry**
Grade 5	• Write and interpret numerical expressions. • Analyze patterns and relationships.	• Understand the place-value system. • Perform operations with multi-digit whole numbers and with decimals to the hundredths.	• Use equivalent fractions as a strategy to add and subtract fractions. • Apply and extend previous understandings of multiplication and division to multiply and divide fractions.	• Convert like measurement units within a given measurement system. • Represent and interpret data. • Geometric measurement: understand concepts of volume and relate volume to multiplication and to addition.	• Graph points on the coordinate plane to solve real-world and mathematical problems. • Classify two-dimensional figures into categories based on their properties.

References

Barnett, Janet H. "A Brief History of Algorithms in Mathematics." In *The Teaching and Learning of Algorithms in School Mathematics,* edited by Lorna J. Morrow, pp. 69–77. Reston, Va.: National Council of Teachers of Mathematics, 1998.

Burns, Marilyn. *About Teaching Mathematics: A K–8 Resource,* 2nd ed. Sausalito, Calif.: Math Solutions, 2000.

Campbell, Patricia. Project IMPACT: Increasing Mathematics Power for All Children and Teachers. Phase 1, Final Report. College Park, Md.: Center for Mathematics Education, University of Maryland, 1995.

Carraher, David W., Mara M. Martinez, and Analúcia D. Schliemann. "Early Algebra and Mathematical Generalization." *ZDM—The International Journal on Mathematics Education* 40 (2008): 3–22.

Carraher, David W., Analúcia D. Schliemann, and Judah Schwartz. "Early Algebra is Not the Same as Algebra Early." In *Algebra in the Early Grades*, edited by James J. Kaput, David W. Carraher, and Maria L. Blanton, pp. 235–72. Mahwah, N.J.: Lawrence Erlbaum Associates, 2008.

Carpenter, Thomas P., Linda Levi, Megan L. Franke, and Julie K. Zeringue. "Algebra in Elementary School: Developing Relational Thinking." *ZDM—The International Journal on Mathematics Education* 37 (2005): 53–59.

The Common Core Standards Writing Team. *Progressions for the Common Core Standards.* WordPress.com. 2011.

Curcio, Frances R. *Developing Data-graph Comprehension in Grades K–8,* 3rd ed. Reston, Va.: National Council of Teachers of Mathematics, 2010.

DeGuire, Linda J. "Pólya Visits the Classroom." In *Problem Solving in School Mathematics,* 1980 Yearbook of the National Council of Teachers of Mathematics (NCTM), edited by Stephen Kulik, pp. 70–79. Reston, Va.: NCTM, 1980.

DiME. "Culture, Race, Power, and Mathematics Education." In *Handbook of Research on Mathematics Teaching and Learning*, 2nd ed., edited by Frank K. Lester, Jr., pp. 405–33. Charlotte, N.C.: Information Age Publishing, 2007.

Earnest, Darrell. "Supporting Generative Thinking about Number Lines, the Cartesian Plane, and Graphs of Linear Functions." Dissertation, University of California, Berkeley. Ann Arbor: ProQuest/UMI, 2012. (Publication No. 3555658).

Earnest, Darrell, and Aadina Balti. "Instructional Strategies for Grade 3 Algebra: Results of a Research-Practice Collaboration." *Teaching Children Mathematics* 14 (2008): 518–22.

Fosnot, Catherine T., and Maarten Dolk. *Young Mathematicians at Work: Constructing Multiplication and Division.* Portsmouth, N.H.: Heinemann, 2001.

González, Norma, Rosi Andrade, Marta Civil, and Luis Moll. "Bridging Funds of Distributed Knowledge: Creating Zones of Practices in Mathematics. *Journal of Education for Students Placed at Risk* 6 (2001): 115–32.

Griffin, Sharon A., Robbie Case, and Robert S. Siegler. "Rightstart: Providing the Central Conceptual Prerequisites for First Formal Learning of Arithmetic to Students at Risk for School Failure." In *Classroom Lessons: Integrating Cognitive Theory and Classroom Practice,* edited by Kate McGilly, pp. 25–49. Cambridge, Mass.: MIT Press, 1994.

Henderson, Kenneth B., and Robert E. Pingry. "Problem-Solving in Mathematics." In *The Learning of Mathematics: Its Theory and Practice,* 1953 Yearbook of the National Council of Teachers of Mathematics (NCTM), edited by Howard F. Fehr, pp. 228–70. Washington, D.C.: NCTM, 1953.

Knapp, Michael S., Nancy E. Adelman, Camille Marder, Heather McCollum, Margaret C. Needels, Christine Padilla, Patrick M. Shields, Brenda J. Turnbull, and Andrew A. Zucker. *Teaching for Meaning in High-Poverty Schools.* New York: Teachers College Press, 1995.

Lave, Jean, and Etienne Wenger. *Situated Learning: Legitimate Peripheral Participation.* Cambridge: Cambridge University Press, 1991.

Lesh, Richard, and Judith Zawojewski. "Problem Solving and Modeling." In *Second Handbook of Research on Mathematics Teaching and Learning,* edited by Frank K. Lester, Jr., pp. 763–804. Charlotte, N.C., and Reston, Va.: Information Age Publishing and National Council of Teachers of Mathematics, 2007.

Lester, Frank K., and Paul E. Kehle. "From Problem Solving to Modeling: The Evolution of Thinking about Research on Complex Mathematical Activity." In *Beyond Constructivism*, edited by Richard Lesh and Helen M. Doerr, pp. 501–17. Mahwah, N.J.: Lawrence Erlbaum Associates, 2003.

Martin, Danny B. "Mathematics Learning and Participation as Racialized Forms of Experience: African American Parents Speak on the Struggle for Mathematics Literacy." *Mathematical Thinking and Learning* 8 (2006): 197–229.

Mathematics Teaching and Learning to Teach. "Mamadou Half Rectangle." In *DeepBlue*, September 28, 2010. Retrieved October 23, 2012, from http://deepblue.lib.umich.edu/handle/2027.42/78024.

Mathews, Louise. *Gator Pie.* New York: Dodd Mead, 1979.

Moll, Luis, Cathy Amanti, Deborah Neff, and Norma Gonzalez. "Funds of Knowledge for Teaching: A Qualitative Approach to Developing Strategic Connections between Homes and Classrooms." *Theory into Practice* 31 (1992): 132–41.

National Council of Teachers of Mathematics (NCTM). *An Agenda for Action.* Reston, Va.: NCTM, 1980.

———. "Grades 3–5, Lesson 1: A Fraction Activity." Illuminations.nctm.org/Reflections_3-5.html.

———. Essential Understanding Series. Reston, Va.: NCTM, 2010–13.

———. *Making It Happen: A Guide to Interpreting and Implementing* Common Core State Standards for Mathematics. Reston, Va.: NCTM, 2011.

———. *Principles and Standards for School Mathematics.* Reston, Va.: NCTM, 2000.

———. Reasoning and Sense Making Series. Reston, Va.: NCTM, 2009–10.

National Governors Association Center for Best Practices and Council of Chief State School Officers (NGA Center and CCSSO). *Common Core State Standards for Mathematics.* Washington, D.C.: NGA Center and CCSSO, 2010. http://www.corestandards.org.

National Research Council. *Adding It Up: Helping Children Learn Mathematics.* Washington D.C.: National Academy Press, 2001.

O'Daffer, Phares, ed. *Problem Solving: Tips for Teachers.* Reston, Va.: NCTM, 1988.

Pollak, Henry. "Introduction: What Is Mathematical Modeling?" In *Mathematical Modeling Handbook*, edited by Heather Gould, Diane R. Murray, and Andrew Sanfratello, pp. vii–xi. Bedford, Mass.: COMAP, 2011.

Pólya, George. *How to Solve It,* 2nd ed. Princeton, N.J.: Princeton University Press, 1957.

Russell, Susan Jo, Deborah Schifter, and Virginia Bastable. *Connecting Arithmetic to Algebra: Strategies for Building Algebraic Thinking in the Elementary Grades.* Portsmouth, N.H.: Heinemann, 2012.

Saxe, Geoffrey B., Meghan M. Shaughnessy, Ann Shannon, Jennifer M. Langer-Osuna, Ryan Chinn, and Maryl Gearhart. "Learning about Fractions as Points on a Number Line." In *The Learning of Mathematics,* 2007 Yearbook of the National Council of Teachers of Mathematics, edited by W. Gary Martin, Marilyn E. Strutchens, and Portia C. Elliott, pp. 221–37. Reston, Va.: NCTM, 2007.

Schoenfeld, Alan H. "Problem Solving in the United States, 1970–2008: Research and Theory, Practice and Politics." *ZDM—The International Journal on Mathematics Education* 39 (2007): 537–51.

Schwartz, Sydney L. *Implementing the Common Core State Standards through Mathematical Problem Solving: Kindergarten–Grade 2.* Reston, Va.: National Council of Teachers of Mathematics, 2013.

Silver, Edward A., and Mary Kay Stein. "The QUASAR Project: The 'Revolution of the Possible' in Mathematics Instructional Reform in Urban Middle Schools." *Urban Education* 30 (1996): 476–521.

TERC. *Investigations in Number, Data, and Space,* 2nd ed. Upper Saddle River, N.J.: Pearson, 2007.

Van de Walle, John, Karen Karp, and Jennifer Bay-Williams. *Elementary and Middle School Mathematics: Teaching Developmentally,* 7th ed. New York: Pearson, 2010.